Inspiration

vs

Motivation

Abundant Life or Abundant Strife

by

Patrick Corn

DEDICATION

To all of the men and women who have inspired me spiritually,
musically, and each so abundantly.
Thank you for all you have done for me.

May His peace be yours, and His blessings abound without measure.

And to my bride

Monica Lynne Corn

An inspiration to me and everyone who meets her
The one who models this book every day

CONTENTS

About The Author

Presentations

ACKNOWLEDGMENTS

Thelma Kilpatrick Corn
My mother who gave me life and taught me how to live it.
Her humor and her pain taught me much about living.

Geraldine Wyatt
The foundation of my musical career whose instruction sat
me apart and made me a player, not just a picker.

Joyce Hubbard Carpenter
My "surrogate mother" who birthed in me a desire for
musical sufficiency, not just proficiency. Her love for Christ
guided me through treacherous waters and quickened my heart
to the leading of the Holy Spirit.

Alex Houston
My oldest and dearest friend who continually encouraged me to reach
out and realize my dreams. His kindness and love for Christ
always demonstrated the Fruit Of The Spirit.

Carl Sandburg
Mr. Sandburg taught me my first guitar chord when I was
only seven years old. His continued interest in me, a little
mountain boy encouraged me and challenged me.
He caused me to embrace effective communication.

Faye Smith
Her love for the Lord and spirit of true worship
was demonstrated so beautifully in my darkest hour
causing me to hunger for a worship-filled lifestyle.

The Holy Spirit
Awakens me at the oddest hours to impart the Father's
desires for my love and ministry to the body of Christ.

1 CHOICES

I n the words of that great philosopher and country music singer George Jones: Lyrics by Billy Wayne Yates and Michael Curtis

"I've had choices since the day that I was born.
I've heard voices that told me right from wrong.
If I had listened I wouldn't be here today,
Living and dying with the choices I've made."

It has been said that the quality of anyone's life is the sum total of the choices he or she makes. In his book "Attitude" Christian author Chuck Swindoll, he states that the quality of one's life is "10 percent of what happens to you and 90 percent of how you react to it." Our choices do determine the course of our lives, but the question looms, "How do I make correct choices in a world that has blurred those lines so intensely?" That is a very valid question in that society today appears to be fulfilling the prophecy that "in the last days..." (2Timothy 3) Good has become evil, and evil has become good. This is a dilemma that we face moment by moment, and day by day.

So, what do we do to ensure that we make the right choices? It is my deepest desire that this book will give you a Biblical method and a Biblical standard that will enable you to instantly facilitate every choice or decision that you may encounter. This method of guidance should enable you to "test the Spirit" (1John 4) with deadly accuracy and conquer the "illusion of confusion" that the world imposes upon us.

Every single thing we think, do, or say comes from one of two promptings; *Inspiration* or *Motivation*. It is your choice.

We are either *inspired* to perform certain actions or we are *motivated* to perform certain actions. The general thought is that *"Inspiration"* and *"Motivation"* are synonymous when, in fact, they are diametrically opposed. *Inspiration* comes from *within* you and *motivation* comes from *without*. Choices that are prompted by the Spirit within produce one type of fruit and choices prompted from *without* will produce another type of fruit. This is the beginning our journey together. How do these two terms differ? How do we discern the difference? How do I choose?

Let's take a look at the word *Inspiration.*

The root word of inspiration is *"spirit."* We receive inspiration from the prompting of the Spirit that is within us. This prompting is commonly known as *unction*, *gut feeling*, or *inkling*. We receive the prompting from the Holy Spirit causing us to be *inspired* to perform certain actions. Actions that are *inspired* always produce the Fruit Of The Spirit. In all honesty, the spirit within you may not be the *Holy Spirit*. Always listen to your stomach! It can give you more than just hunger pangs!

This "Spirit" concern is a pivotal point in our journey together. At this moment you must determine what kind of spirit actually resides within you. To make this determination, it requires complete personal honesty. Take an inventory of whom and what you honestly know yourself to be. The prevailing question to be answered is this: Is the spirit within me the Holy Spirit or is there another spirit residing within me? This answer is absolutely critical to your success in making the correct choices in life.

The reason your answer is so vital is the dynamic of "cause and effect." Unless the Holy Spirit resides within you, it is absolutely ludicrous to expect the Fruit of the Spirit to be evident in the choices that you will make. Quite frankly, this book will be totally useless to you. You will have a distorted and frustrated view of the entire process.

The choice to embrace the Holy Spirit to reside within you is the most critical choice you will ever make. It is an *eternal choice*.

Inspired choices must be the result of the prompting of the Holy Spirit whose actions always produce the Fruit Of The Spirit, as described in Galatians 5:22-23. "Against these things, there is no law." Freedom follows as we benefit from these gifts:

Peace

Love

Joy

Gentleness

Meekness

Kindness

Goodness

Patience

Truth

Self-Control

Note that the scripture expresses a very important fact; "Against these things, there is no law." As a result, an inspired choice is ALWAYS the right choice. There is no argument about it. The Holy Spirit will not, and cannot, guide you to a choice that doesn't glorify God. It is an absolute impossibility.

The Lord tells us that he will "never leave us or forsake us" and He also says that he will never "tempt us." With those facts in mind, how then could He ever lead us to a choice that would do anything but glorify Him? It cannot be both ways without undermining who He says He is. We can rest in His promise that "if you abide in Me, I will abide in you."

He is "the Lord thy God who is your righteousness"; Jehovah -Tsidkenu (Jeremiah23:6)

Now, in contrast, let's take a close look at the word *Motivation*.

The root word of motivation is *motive*. Motivated choices benefit or glorify someone other than God and His kingdom. *Motivated* choices are not from *within*, but from *without*, when we respond to man or circumstances. There is always a hidden agenda behind a motivated choice. Someone is going to benefit from the *motivated* choice. That "someone" could be our self or another wanting to utilize our talents or giftings for their own benefit.

Motivated choices, in time, always produce the fruit of the flesh which is described in Galatians 23:19-21

Hatred
Discord
Dissension
Factions
Jealousy
Envy
Fits Of Rage
Selfish Ambition
Addictions
Immorality

"As I have told you before, those who live like this
will not inherit the kingdom of God."

If we are the *motivator*, we are manipulating others to benefit ourselves in many possible ways; financial gain, power, control, prestige, emotional blackmail, self-interest, or just pure ole meanness. Someone will gain at another's expense in a motivated circumstance. Motivators only "give to get." *Motivated* choices will never be the inspired result of the Spirit within us, but from a spirit without, perpetuated by man and circumstance.

Once again, this is a moment to pause and take that personal inventory mentioned previously. What spirit really does lives within you? If that spirit is "driving" you, then it is not the Holy Spirit. The Holy Spirit only guides" you to the glorifying results of your choices.

If you have determined that it is not the Holy Spirit living within you, then you will be unable to utilize the dynamics that follow in this text in any way. Your future efforts will be of no consequence whatsoever. It is impossible to have it both ways. It is not just a matter of changing your attitude, but a matter of changing your heart. Let's look closely at how *motivation* impacts people.

If you are like most, you have grown up thinking that *motivation* is a great thing. Coaches *motivate* the team in the locker room and on the field. Why? To win! Cheerleaders *motivate* the crowd. Why? To pump the crowd up and cheer the *motivated* players, *motivated* by the coach, who is *motivated* by the administration to win in order to satisfy the egos of the Booster Club who are *motivated* by their personal pride in winning and becoming #1! Reality Check! Only God is #1! He has no intention of sharing His glory with anyone or any organization.

Of course, it is great to win, and we are truly called to *excellence*, but a true winner has the desire *within* to do whatever it takes to glorify God first in everything that he or she does. That's a true winner! Let me give you an example of "Great Intentions," or so we think. Picture this...

It is early on Monday morning and time for the weekly sales meeting at the HotShot Motor Company. The sales staff files slowly into the training room with heads bowed; not from reverence, but from the burden of dread for the upcoming week. As they all slowly sit down, the din of the negative conversations begins to rise until Mr. Ross, the dealer, walks into the room with the new incentive plan for the week that, in his mind, will turn their negative attitudes into a huge positive. Thrusting out his arm and fist, and in his best leadership cheering voice, shouts with great exuberance, the usual motivational cheer. He thinks it will really get the sales staff pumped up and excited. RIGHT!

"How do you feel?" he shouts! The staff responds, "Happy!" "How do you feel?" The staff responds "Healthy!" The dealer shouts, "How do you win?" The staff responds half-heartedly, "Sell!" He repeats louder, "How do you win?" The staff shouts somewhat louder, "Sell!"

Feeling quite elated, Mr. Ross glows with his winning smile. He is so happy! He is so proud of his dynamic leadership!

He is about to offer these salespeople an incentive program that will blow their minds. The atmosphere is about to be supercharged with enthusiasm when they find out what he is about to do for them.

"Folks, I have designed a contest this week that you are going to love! Every person in this room will want to win this contest. It is huge! It is exciting! It is a dream- come- true for you all. Are you ready? Ok! Now here is how the new contest works..."

The dealer begins to lay out the terms of the incentive program with great care as he leans in as though he is about to unveil a secret of national importance, "Ok! Here is the deal. From 10 AM today through this Saturday at 9 PM, the salesperson who makes the largest total gross profit on their units sold will win an all-expense paid trip to Atlanta, flying there on a private jet, with $1000 cash to spend any way you might want. You'll be picked up by a limo at the airport and whisked to the Omni Hotel where you, and your significant other, with spend the entire weekend in a palatial suite. Saturday evening the limo will take you to a Braves game where you will view the game from a skybox just over the infield. The skybox will be complete with a sandwich bar and any beverage you can imagine. After the game, the limo will take you on a tour of the downtown Atlanta night spots where you will choose the club you would like to spend the rest of the evening. At midnight the limo will arrive to escort you back to the hotel. On Sunday afternoon the private jet will return you home in time for plenty of rest before the sales meeting the next Monday. Isn't that exciting? Can you believe it?"

WOW! What a deal, right? Mr. Ross thinks he has them so fired up that he'll have to hose them down. Little does he know that the second they walk out of the door, a downward spiral will ensue for the majority of the sales staff. In short order, the sheets of paper outlining the fabulous incentive program will begin to fill the wastebaskets at each sales desk.

The first thing to occur is the sales staff will splinter into factions with their own ideas of what the incentive plan means to them personally. Super-Spiritual Sammy says, "If it's God's will, I will win."Fred says to Ed, old-timers there at the dealership, "Aw, my wife would never fly on a plane. This deal doesn't mean a thing to me." Then they mope around all day, with a prime opportunity to gripe and groan.

Bud, Joe, and Jay agree, "That plan doesn't turn my crank! I don't even like the Braves. Now, if it was professional football, I'd go for it!"

Brenda and Shirley (both single mothers) congregate, "I couldn't go on a trip like this one. I'd never trust a babysitter with my kids for a whole weekend. I just get so mad when he puts out an incentive program like that. It's just for the men anyway, and besides, I don't even have a significant other."

Kevin, a young newlywed, hits the lot with a vengeance catching every customer that comes on the lot. He wants to win that trip! His new bride would really enjoy it. He's going to do everything possible to win. He's going to win! His energy level is twice that of anyone in the dealership. He wants to be the hero at the dealership and at home.

Now, Terry and Chuck are seasoned car salesmen, and they begin to grumble that Kevin is catching every customer that hits the lot and they can't outrun him. They decide to alternate calling Kevin to the phone for a call (that doesn't even exist) when they see a customer drive on the lot. That will give them an edge on getting out to the new potential buyer. Why they can't get a chance to even finish their coffee or the morning paper. They hate programs like this. They are more interested in the ballgames that their grandkids play. After all, they spend at least four hours a day discussing those games and the bad calls the umpires made. They'll survive without the incentive plan. They always do!

Simon and Keith complain that they would rather have a check for the expense that the old man is putting out for this incentive. They aren't interested in going to Atlanta, and they don't even like the Braves. In their opinion the whole thing is ridiculous, and they aren't going to even try.

Roberta sees how aggressive Kevin has become on the lot and determines, in her mind, that Kevin just wants to become a sales manager. Robbie knows that she should be the promoted to that position, even though she is an ardent clock watcher, never misses a lunch or smoke break, appears constantly angry, and never follows up with her customers. She knows how to run the dealership better than anyone. Roberta has paid her dues, and she deserves a promotion.

7

Incentive Plan... *Dead On Arrival*! Why? It is a *motivated* plan from the very onset. Was the dealer truly interested in doing something great for his employees? Absolutely not! Only one person could benefit from the concerted effort of the staff as a whole...*Sales Motivation*! DOA!

Was Mr. Ross responding to the Spirit within him or the circumstances without? He put the plan in place to incentivize the staff to sell more cars as a group and simply make the dealership more money. The plan is only a carrot to dangle before the staff to cause them to synergistically produce more income for him....*Highly Motivated*! He is only *giving to get*; a typical managerial mistake. He has to pay for those commercials!

The plan produced the *fruit of the flesh* in various forms throughout the entire staff; hatred, discord, dissension, fits of rage, envy, imaginations, supposition, grumbling, complaining, manipulation, and selfish ambition. Mr. Ross's plan was doomed from the start. It will never work! DOA!

Now, if Kevin had gotten up one morning and lovingly decided, "You know, I just love my new bride. I'd love to take her to Atlanta and see a Braves game. Maybe we could stay at the Omni Hotel, do some shopping, and enjoy some of the Atlanta restaurant scenes. I'd love to do that. I believe I am going to work extra hard over the next few weeks and sell a lot of cars to meet my goal. I'll be her hero! I'm on it!"

If Kevin were *inspired* to do that loving act, as a result of the Spirit within him, not a word would have ever been said by his co-workers concerning his aggressive work habits. It would have probably just been perceived as Kevin just having a "great week." Perhaps they would have even praised his zeal as a newlywed trying to jump-start the financial state of their new marriage. None of the above-fractured scenarios would have existed because Kevin would have been *inspired* not *motivated*. He would have simply operated under the laws of "seed, time, and harvest," born of inspiration, energized by the power of the Holy Spirit, and working hard to realize his personal goal."

Now, that is a winning combination! *Inspiration with zeal*!

The dealer presented a self-serving plan to manipulate the staff to act solely on his behalf. It may have looked good on paper, but it lacked the key ingredient for true success.... *Inspiration*!

Are you an *inspiration* to those around you or are you a motivating manipulator? Perhaps you are the brunt of a motivator's tactics, finding yourself constantly on the defense as to the intentions of those who impact your life dramatically? Who are these people?

Your Spouse
Your Children
Family Members
Your Employer
Coworkers
Church Family or Staff

In the following pages, you will discover that *Inspiration* and *Motivation* are truly diametrically opposed and that these two promptings will shape your future resulting in abundant life or abundant strife. This following information will provide a very simple way to "test the Spirit" from within and from without, as to every decision you will encounter. You will learn to overcome *Motivation* with *Inspiration*. Your *inspired* choices will change your life and bring you peace and glorify God.

Each of the following chapters will contrast the *Fruit of the Spirit* (Inspiration) and the *fruit of the flesh* (Motivation). The ultimate goal is for you to be able to immediately determine what you should think, do, or say in response to the motivating circumstances that come your way.

You will gain great discernment; Spirit-led wisdom that will change your life and the lives of others around you.

Just as important is that you will put your own actions in check that could identify you as a *motivator*. Are you *inspired* by your actions and desires or are you *motivated* by your actions and desires? Do you *give to get*? That is always a horrible investment.

Let's begin our journey as we discover the benefits of *Inspiration* and the ramifications of *Motivation*.

This process is a lifestyle that will enable you to heartily embrace your future without fear, as you work to achieve your heart's desires. This process can determine the quality and value of your life, and those around you, on a daily basis. Choose to be inspired!

Do you want abundant life or abundant strife? It is simply your choice!

"Take delight in the LORD, and he will give you the desires of your heart."
(Psalm 37:4)

2 PEACE VS FEAR

INSPIRATION....PEACE

I've met very few people in my life and ministry who didn't long for a lifestyle of peace. I could dare say that when asked the question, "What is your greatest desire?" One of the top three answers would undoubtedly be *Peace*. There is a deep longing to live in peace.

It's a fairly common joke that in a beauty pageant that when the above question is asked of a contestant her will answer will be, "World peace." Sorry sweetie, it will never happen. As noble as that answer might be, world peace is not ordained by God. "Well, that's not very encouraging," you say? "But, I have a bumper sticker that says "COEXIST." Can't we all just get along? Nope! It's not going to happen!

Let's step back in time to an encounter that a young Egyptian slave girl named Hagar had while she was hiding in the desert. Hagar was a slave to Abram's wife, Sarai. This historical account is found in Genesis 16. This timeframe is before Abram became Abraham, and Sarai became Sarah.

After many years of trying, Sarai was unable to give Abram a child. Sarai then gave Hagar to Abram to be a wife so that his lineage might begin. Abram slept with Hagar, and she conceived a child with him. When Hagar realized she was pregnant, she began to despise Sarai. Sarai goes to Abram and blames him for the misery she is suffering at the hand of

Hagar. I suppose two "wrongs "really don't make a "right."

"You are responsible for the wrong I am suffering. I put my slave in your arms, and now that she knows she is pregnant, she despises me. May the LORD judge between you and me."
(Genesis 16:4-5)

Wait a minute! Hold the phone! Now I may be wrong, but I do believe Sarai was the one who put this situation in motion, right? Now she is blaming Abram for the fact that Hagar despises her? Abram tells Sarai to deal with Hagar as she pleases, so Sarai begins to mistreat Hagar badly. Hagar eventually has endured enough abuse and fled to the desert; where she encounters the angel of the Lord. The angel asks....

"Hagar, slave of Sarai, where have you come from, and where are you going?" "I'm running away from my mistress Sarai," she answered. Then the angel of the LORD told her, "Go back to your mistress and submit to her." The angel added, "I will increase your descendants so much that they will number like the sands of the desert."
(Genesis 16:9-10)

The angel of the LORD then said to her:

"You are now pregnant, and you will give birth to a son. You shall name him Ishmael for the LORD has heard of your misery. He will be a wild donkey of a man; his hand will be against everyone and everyone's hand against him, and he will live in hostility toward all his brothers."
(Genesis 16:11-12)

Did you catch that last part of each of those phrases? The Lord will increase the descendants to a *number beyond measure* (phrase 1), that there would be *constant fighting*, and he and his descendants would be in *constant conflict with his brothers and their descendants* (phrase 2).

Who were his brothers? Half brothers Issac and Jacob were the sons that Sarah eventually bore, fathered by Abraham (Israel).

The descendants of Ishmael and the descendants of Issac and Jacob have been in constant conflict for centuries past to this present day, and *world peace* will never happen.

That being said, "What peace should I expect through *inspired* choices?" Let's go to the source of our peace for that answer.

Through our lives of *Inspiration,* the peace that we find is in solely in our Heavenly Father. He states, *"I am the Lord thy God who IS your peace."* [Emphasis mine] He is Jehovah-Shalom. He doesn't just give us peace; He IS our peace. Our relationship of trust and faith in Him gives us the peace we need to contend with any circumstance. He is the only real peace we will ever know. I love the lyrics to this gospel music chorus;

> "The only real peace that I find, dear Lord is in You.
> The only real peace that I find, dear Lord is in You.
> Through all life's frustrations, I need You, Lord I know I do
> Because the only real peace that I find, dear Lord is in You."
> (The Hemphills – 1981)

We will never find peace in anything temporal. Peace will not come from any situation or institution on this earth. The entirety of our world is subject to change in a matter of seconds through "cause and effect." Wealth creates its own set of problems. Health is subjected to change in the blink of an eye. Relationships are in need of perpetual maintenance. The only thing in life that is constant... is *change.*

Nature or the Universe hasn't the capacity to provide us with real peace. We may feel "peaceful" while enjoying a natural habitat, but the peace we sincerely long for can only be found through an intimate relationship with the Creator of both the universe and nature. God created the universe and the forces of nature that are found within it. The universe is merely a living space and nature provides the amenities that provide our ability to exist physically, but not spiritually. We are subjected to the forces within in the universe and nature, thus we are subjected to those influences as a mandate without a relationship. His peace is a matter of a relationship which is delivered to us by the Holy Spirit. The universe or nature never sacrificed their earthly existence for your benefit. From Jesus' own lips he says,

"Peace I leave with you; my peace I give you.
I do not give to you as the world gives.
Do not let your hearts be troubled and do not be afraid."
(John 14:27)

MOTIVATION....FEAR

When we succumb to *motivated* choices, the immediate result is fear. As believers, we are not given a spirit of fear. We should immediately recognize that what we are about to think, we say, or we do, is the wrong thing. Yes! It is that simple! Fear and doubt are first cousins, and they run together like thieving partners. The Spirit within you will guide you and dispel those fears. Fear is the enemy of God's love.

The Bible tells us that "perfect love casts out all fear." (1 John 4:18) Well, let's read that in reverse; "Fear casts out perfect love." Fear causes compromise. When we make choices that are *motivated* by fear, we can rest assured that our sense of peace will quickly vanish as the fear and doubt creep in and overwhelms us. We will second guess our decision as that uneasy feeling will creep in, and we will become unstable, lacking confidence and direction in our thoughts and actions.

Again, a *motivated* choice is a response to *man and circumstance*. Many of our most destructive mistakes are the responses to fearful circumstances. Those situations arrive in a myriad of ways. Quite often the fear that causes our poor choice is very subtle. Our fears may not be a strong storyline for a horror movie script, but fear can be quietly influential, keeping us off-balance, as does a tiny rock in our shoe which prevents our steps to be taken in a normal uncompromised fashion.

These outside influences can immobilize us when we are fearful. Now, I am not talking about a *genuine concern*. Genuine concern is actually a prompting for an *inspired* action causing us to embrace an opportunity to serve others. The response method that we choose will be the key ingredient to maintaining true peace which will overcome the fear that might arise as a result of *motivation* by man and circumstance.

Genuine concern results in a prayerful petition to God which produces peace in our heart and mind. We will be completely confident that He will handle it. These are expected results when we "cast our cares upon Him." (1 Peter 5:7) If we follow through, casting our cares on him, we should not be driven by fear or be anxious at all. We should be resting in the full knowledge that He will handle the situation to His perfect conclusion. Remember, we must lay our troubles at His feet and not go back and pick them up again! Cast your cares upon Him. Let them die! By all means, do not worry! The only thing that worry will change is the worrier. Talk about expending worthless energy! Worrying is a perfectly worthless exercise. It never builds up. It only tears down.

*"Therefore I tell you, do not worry about your life, what you will eat or drink; or about your body, what you will wear. Is not life more than food and the body more than clothes? Look at the birds of the air; they do not sow or reap or store away in barns, and yet your heavenly Father feeds them. Are you not much more valuable than they? Can anyone of you by **worry**ing add a single hour to your life?"*
(Matt 6:25-34)

Worry is well-disguised fear wrapped in well-meaning wrapping paper. Let's take a look at some of those *motivating* circumstances that do cause the fear-ridden choices. These circumstances will hold our lives hostage.

Financial Matters
Marriage Problems
Being Alone
Family Relationships Past and Present
Expectations Of Others
Procrastination
Work-Related Relationships
Job Security
Memories Of The Past
The Fear Of The Future
Self Image and Self Worth
Health Concerns
Addictions
Hobbies
Spiritual Security
Political Concerns
Imaginations and Supposition
Fantasy

If we make fearful choices prompted by man or outside circumstances, you can count on a negative result. If one has to be "driven" to do the most common things, you can be assured there will be negative results. Oh, what loss we experience when we make our choices in response to fear. One of the most revealing lessons I ever learned about fear was through a young man who was a sales manager at a car dealership.

I don't know if I had ever met a more disagreeable person in my life. This guy was a total jerk. How he was ever elevated to his position remains an absolute mystery to me. He was certainly no people person.

I was in the process of preparing a sermon that I would deliver on the upcoming Sunday. The subject was "Fear." I thought it might be revealing to ask several people in the dealership a simple question, "What is your greatest fear?" That exercise was very revealing.

I had already asked that question to several folks and received answers that I fully expected; the fear of losing their job, the fear of their parents dying, the fear of losing their children, the fear of catastrophic illness, and the like. I basically ignored the young sales manager as I rarely conversed with him about anything unless it was absolutely required. But then I thought, "I just wonder what that jerk's greatest fear would be? What do I have to lose? I'll just ask him!"

I walked up to his perch by the front window, where he kept a close eye on the lot traffic and the salespeople attending to the customers. I sat down in a chair and asked, while he still had his back to me, "Stephen, I'm doing a message at my church this Sunday. The subject is 'Fear.' I've asked several folks here in the dealership what their greatest fear might be. Stephen, what is your greatest fear?"

There was a rather long pause until he spun slowly in his chair and looked at me with tears welling up in his eyes saying, "That's an easy one...the fear of being alone." That answer stunned me. He continued, "I know exactly what you are thinking. Due to my personality and the way that I treat people, I virtually ensure that I will always be alone. But, you don't understand what 'being alone' means to a person like me. It doesn't mean that I am by myself. I can be in a room with a hundred people and still be totally alone. 'Alone' to me is when I enter into a relationship with someone and then when it fails; I am 'alone.'

The problem with people like me is that I will make sure the relationship eventually fails. I will leave before I am left."

I don't know of a time dealing with the auto industry that I was more surprised. That insight gave me more empathy for folks who are so disagreeable and in pain. It gave validation to the old adage,

"Rudeness is a weak person's imitation of strength."

I became Stephen's only friend in the entire dealership, and I would never let him sabotage our relationship. Oh, he tried, but Stephen never won. He was stuck with me.....never alone.

I must admit that he never returned a phone call after I left the dealership. I suppose he was "alone" after all.

3 JOY VS DISCORD

INSPIRATION.... JOY

If you ever have the opportunity to meet my wife Monica, you will encounter an individual who truly expresses the joy of the Lord. Her joy-filled enthusiasm is the light of anyone's day. What a perfect person to serve as the receptionist at our church. The first face that anyone encounters when they walk into the lobby of the church is Monica; dancing eyes, bubbly vivacious personality, a very tender and compassionate heart, and an infectious giggle that could easily be a ringtone. She greets every individual as if they were a long-lost friend.

No matter what temperament the guest might possess at the time they enter the lobby, I can assure you that when they leave, they'll be in a better frame of mind from just being in the lobby with Monica. She is truly *inspiring*. She has to be one of the most loved individuals I know.

At one point in her long history as the receptionist, a new executive pastor was brought in to the church staff. He had retired from a very prominent church in West Tennessee and was recruited to assist the Senior Pastor at that time. Shortly after his arrival, he mandated that all of the staff would be required to take a drug test. That type of test was becoming somewhat of a standard order of procedure for many businesses and institutions at the time. Monica had no concern about taking a drug test at all.

Of course, the very first person scheduled to have their drug test would be Monica. She willingly complied, and her results proved that she had no drugs in her system. That was never the first concern at all. The odd thing was that to her knowledge; no other staff member was ever scheduled to take a drug test after her. Humm?? It became our supposition that perhaps the new pastor thought that she was on something that made her so vivacious and bubbly. Perhaps he had never seen the "joy of the Lord" before! Now, that is just our supposition, but it sure makes sense. Having passed her drug test, that new pastor coined a cute nickname for her that expressed his pride in her passing the test. He became a believer! She was clean! Oh the joy of the Lord!

People who make *inspired* choices have a perfect right to be joyful. They never have to be concerned with negative results simply because "against these things, there is no law." Monica never had a moment's concern about her drug test because she knew that she had nothing to hide. *Inspired* choices promote the joy of the Lord in our lives, ensuring that we will never have to look over our shoulder to see if doom is creeping up on us. We gain inner-peace and confidence that fosters a warm feeling of security that makes *inspiration* very inviting.

"The joy of the Lord is your strength." (Nehemiah 8:10) Strength and confidence are to be enjoyed when we know that we are *inspired* by our choices moment by moment. It is as if we experience small victories throughout the entire day. That realization alone should inspire each of us, as the joy of the Lord floods our life and spills over to those around us. What a lifestyle!

Joy and happiness are not the same things. Joy comes from within and happiness from without. Happiness is simply the satisfaction level to which we rise to as a result of our "happenings." Joy filled individuals can be in the midst of some dire circumstances, and you may never know it. Joy filled individuals are trusting in the Lord which does not actually require any input from others.

As the hymn says, "In Christ ALONE I put my trust." (My emphasis)

M OTIVATION.... DISCORD

In contrast to a joy-filled life, the joyless individual creates discord. It is very easy to negatively influence those around you resulting from their *motivated* responses. It seems as though the law of "action and reaction" is quite evident in joyless people; troublemakers!

Joyless people are never satisfied; one way or the other. They become "contrary." Now, there is a word you don't hear very much today.

I was raised in the country in Western North Carolina in the small town of Hendersonville, NC. Like any small town, there are communities with certain *contrary* "characters" as residents. Our community had the usual cast of characters; the nosey old lady, the pious churchgoer, the snooty one rich lady, the local drunks, a nut-case or two, the school teacher that was old as dirt, the local country store proprietor, the hussy, the bullies, the star athlete, the petty schoolgirls, the men who walked the streets without a job and not wanting one, the gossips, the grumpy old men, and the sleazy preacher. Uh oh! I just realized those were all in MY family! I'm just kidding! No one in our family owned a local store or was a school teacher.

Honestly, I can say that I did grow up thinking that my community might be less than joyful. Many of the characterizations above are the results of joyless lives. Joyless lives create discord by promoting judgmental attitudes, arrogance, slothfulness, hopelessness, various forms of abuse, loneliness, drunkenness, and a lack of enthusiasm. I do realize that the generation before me lived through The Depression and, as a result, they lost a vast amount of their joy, but I was lucky. I had someone who seemed always to be joyful, challenging me to be more than my dreams.

The one person who caused all of the above to fade to black was my mother; Thelma Kilpatrick Corn, aka "Aunt Sal." My Mom was a real live Minnie Pearl. She taught me about living a joy-filled life with her constant display of humor. I do believe that she knew more jokes than anyone I've ever known. Granted, they weren't all appropriate for mixed company, but she knew the limits. She could find humor in just about any situation no matter how dire the circumstance.
Some folks use humor as a hiding place. That was not the case with my Mom. She was truly joyful. She had to be joyful to be so strong.

Her life as a wife and mother gave her the many challenges that could have caused her to be highly *motivated*, but I witnessed her ability to turn things around by making *inspired* choices on the spot.

One of her least favorite people groups were the gossips. She would never "triangulate" about anyone. She always said, "If you can't say something nice, don't say anything at all." Though she bore some terrific burdens, she aptly demonstrated *inspiration to* everyone she ever met, and she was loved for that very fact. I can't recall a time that she ever caused any discord at all. Her tolerance level was amazing. She was a consummate giver until she was "give out"; having given everything that she could to someone or some cause.

Now is a perfect time to revisit that personal inventory again:

Do you cause discord with others because of a joyless life?

Do you look at the world through some distorted glass that makes everything and everyone appear very dark?

Do you add to the lives with whom you associate, or do you drain them of their joy?

Is your attitude such that you are defeated before you even start?

Do you constantly complain and whine about the majority of the circumstances in your home, church, or workplace?

Do you take more than you give? Are you thankful?

Do you "give" only to "get?"

Are you contrary?

If so, the joy of the Lord is your strength... simply make *inspired* choices!

4 GENTLENESS VS DISSENSION

INSPIRATION.... GENTLENESS

In today's world, the term "gentle" bears a connotation of someone who allows him or herself to be perceived as an easy mark for people with aggressive and negative behavioral traits. Being gentle doesn't mean one is soft or indefensible. To treat others or circumstances gently implies that there is a possibility of breakage or damage that should be considered. My "Cornucopian" term for a situation like this is the "Humpty Dumpty Effect." "All the Kings horses and all the King's men couldn't put Humpty Dumpty back together again." What was he doing on the wall in the first place? He must have been *motivated*!

In the South, we call it being "genteel." A person described as genteel always carries a great deal of respect and appreciation in our Southern social structure. They add class to any gathering by demonstrating impeccable manners, an attentive ear, respectfulness, and a gracious attitude.

Gentleness is an essential asset when dealing with personal and business relationships. Quite often a great deal of time, effort, and expense has been invested in developing such a valued relationship. A relationship of this nature calls for great gentleness when decisions, choices if you will, are being considered that could have the potential to cause damage to that relationship.

Gentleness expresses that you care about the health and wellbeing of that relationship and you want to protect it. It is to be handled with great care to avoid breakage.

Gentleness is a form of tender loving care (TLC). Many choices we encounter involve such a dynamic to ensure that, when the final word is said or acted upon, and the deal is struck no damage has been done to cause the relationship to be broken or irreparable. No "recovery time" is needed. The relationship is whole without a nick or single crack.

The one playing field where *gentleness* is on constant call is in the marriage relationship. This is an area where gentleness truly creates strength. For a marriage to be *inspiring* it must be handled with respect, concern, and perpetual care. Mutual respect and unconditional love foster an atmosphere where problems and choices can be resolved with great *gentleness*; no breakage!

Sadly, in this day and time, the institution of marriage is treated without the deep respect that it deserves. A marriage is a choice that should be considered as a lifelong commitment, not just a whimsical tour of the emotions. Our vows are not just "promises," but a "covenant" before God. Promises are easily broken. Sometimes a traffic jam can cause us to break a promise to be home for dinner at a certain time. The weather can cause us to break a promise to be at an important meeting. There are things that we can't control that can cause us to break a promise. We can't manage what we can't control. But a covenant is an entirely different thing. It is not to be broken! A covenant is for life!

When we choose to enter into a covenant, it is a choice that must truly be *inspired*, because a covenant is considered to be irrevocable. One doesn't break a covenant without severe damage to all parties concerned. Breaking a covenant is *never an inspired action*. Such an action is an act that is *fully motivated* and promotes the fruit of the flesh every single time. The spiritual ramifications are immense! Trust me when I say, you will never be able to justify a *motivated reaction* as an *inspired choice*. It will never happen. The Holy Spirit will never *inspire* you to steal another person's spouse!

24

Let's just take a look at what God says about breaking a covenant in Leviticus 26:14:

"If you will not listen to me ... if you spurn my statutes, and if your soul abhors my rules, so that you will not do all my commandments, but **break** *my* **covenant***, then I will do this to you: I will visit you with panic, and wasting disease."*

Nothing *gentle* about that! It's is obvious that God does not take a covenant lightly and nor should we. Again, our marriage vows are not a series of Hallmark promises, but they are a covenant before God and those who witness the making of that covenant. The witness at a marriage ceremony is not there to just witness the signing of the license, but as a witness who can attest to the covenant made between two people.

Perhaps this might be a great time to revisit that personal inventory we have been taking.

Do you consider your marriage to be an inspired covenant with your spouse and God?

Are you *inspirational* or *motivational* in the way you treat your spouse?

Are you acting with *gentleness* toward your spouse considering him or her as a precious item that you refuse to allow to be broken?

It is never too late to be *inspired*. Promote *gentleness* and protect the one you love.

Gentleness is also a very inviting attribute of someone's nature. Gentleness makes you very approachable. You become a conduit for the touch of the Holy Spirit to those around you. If you are genteel, people will gravitate to you because you are inviting. You are not perceived as a threat. After all, if the Holy Spirit imparts that gift to you, in no way will it be reproachable to someone. It will only endear them to you. They will feel safe around you, and they should. After all, the Spirit is present.

MOTIVATION.... DISSENSION

Some of the most easily identifiable Motivational responses are those of *Dissension*. These responses are, without question, the polar opposites of *Gentleness*.

Dissenting individuals utilize strife and conflict to accomplish their self-serving goals. They are contentious and mean-spirited thriving on conflict and quarreling. They are riddled with disharmony and are generally very disagreeable. They are antagonistic by nature. They are unruly. No rules apply to these folks! They are "special!"

People who thrive on dissension are *careless.* They are not careful at all when it comes to relationships. They could *care less*. They think the term "stewardship" is someone on the Love Boat! Their byline is "What's in it for me?" They a are so self-centered that one day they may just turn into a walking navel looking behind themselves in the opposite direction!

Dissenters are professional motivators. The beauty of the situation is that they are easy to spot, and you will spot them quickly. Their actions and attitude are blatant. These folks take great pride that they are brave enough to "speak their mind." Their problem is that they are under the false impression that anyone is even remotely interested in hearing about what they are thinking, or in their opinions. They often take pride in their brash behavior and, in their mind, they are in control. Most people who try to always be *in control* of others are actually quite *out of control* in their own lives. Dissenters impose!

When discerning what is *inspirational* and what is *motivational*, we are given an opportunity to save a great deal of time, trouble, and emotional expense when we choose not to react to the motivation.

Remember... "Ten percent of what happens to you, and ninety percent of how you react to it." Do not let any *motivational* stimuli affect your *inspired* lifestyle. Period! Do not burn a brain cell trying to "understand" the motivator. Don't even try.

If you would like to have *"the peace that passes understanding"* right now, it can be instantaneous. Truly!

"What? No way? I've wanted that my entire adult life!" Well, you are about to have it... You only need to *understand* this one fact:

YOU DO NOT HAVE TO UNDERSTAND EVERYTHING!

Stop trying to figure out everything and analyze everyone. Some situations and some people make absolutely no sense at all. It is not within your job description to figure them out, justify their actions, or validate their behavior. Nor is it within your job description to judge or condemn them. God will handle them in His time IF they will allow Him to work in their lives. It is your job, to prepare yourself to defend your Spirit from the imposition of the *motivational* actions that are thrust toward you. There is no need to place you in harm's way.

*"Finally, be strong in the Lord and in his mighty power. Put on the full armor of God, so that you can take your stand against the devil's schemes. For our struggle is not against flesh and blood, but against the rulers, against the authorities, against the powers **of** this dark world and against the spiritual forces **of** evil in the heavenly realms.*

Therefore, put on the full armor of God, so that when the day of evil comes, you may be able to stand your ground, and after you have done everything, to stand. Stand firm then, with the belt of truth buckled around your waist, with the breastplate of righteousness in place, and with your feet fitted with the readiness that comes from the gospel of peace. In addition to all this, take up the shield of faith, with which you can extinguish all the flaming arrows of the evil one. Take the helmet of salvation and the sword of the Spirit, which is the word of God."
(Ephesians 6:10-17)

"But I might convince them to turn from their wicked ways", you say? Pretty spiritually arrogant aren't you? Once again, is that in your job description? Are you assuming that you will be able to *convince* that person with your eloquence, while the Spirit is trying to *convict*?

Your attempts to *convince* will never trump the Spirit's power to *convict*. If a person isn't *convicted* to alter the course of their life, lasting change will not occur. In all candor, you will actually be *motivating* them as they will simply be responding to man (you) and the circumstance.

"Doesn't that mean I don't care?" Absolutely not! It only means that you must realize your limited ability to change a *motivated life* through your own powers of persuasion. Real change must come from the *conviction* of the Holy Spirit. Then, and only then, will that person be truly *inspirational* rather than *motivational?*

I know that the next suggestion will seem very "non-Christian," but there are times that you just need to leave some folks alone. Leave them alone for your own well being, and create an opportunity to move YOU out of the way enabling them to hear the voice of the Spirit speaking to them. Your zeal may exceed your knowledge. We must remember that the voice of the Spirit is a "still small voice" and it isn't polite to interrupt.

"For we know, brothers and sisters loved by God, that He has chosen you, because our gospel came to you not simply with words but also with power, with the Holy Spirit and deep conviction."
(1Thessalonians 1:4-5)

It is quite natural that we want to make a difference in people's lives but, what difference are we really making? Wouldn't it be truly different if the power of the Holy Spirit could work unencumbered by our personal agenda? We all make "well-meaning mistakes." Our intent is good, but our methods are faulty; filled with logical *reason* offered to an *unreasonable* individual. It is though we are offering a drowning man a drink of water. Resist trying to *convince*. Let the Spirit *convict!*

We are admonished in scripture to leave some people alone. Being alone isn't always a bad scenario. In fact, being left alone will give a greater opportunity for the Spirit to convict. The following scripture might seem harsh, but it is necessary at times to remove yourself from the motivator and the influences provided.

It is not necessary to put yourself in harm's way. Are you vying for martyrdom? Are you attempting a world "cheek turning" record?

"But mark this: There will be terrible times in the last days. People will be lovers of themselves, lovers of money, boastful, proud, abusive, disobedient to their parents, ungrateful, unholy, without love, unforgiving, slanderous, without self-control, brutal, not lovers of the of the good, treacherous, rash, conceited, lovers of pleasure rather than lovers of God— having a form of godliness but denying its power. Have nothing to do with such people."
(2 Timothy 3:1-5)

Did you catch the last line? "Have *nothing to do with such people*." Let the Spirit *convict* the individual of God's desires and precepts. There are times that it is absolutely necessary to remove yourself from the influence of these people. By doing so, you will take yourself out of harm's way and allow the motivator to be alone with God. Then pray fervently that the individual will listen to the still small voice of the Spirit.

And yes, some of those people could be family members and close friends. They are not exempt from being motivators and enablers. At some point, they must be left "alone" with God to their own devices.

"It is to one's honor to avoid strife, but every fool is quick to quarrel."
(Proverbs20:3)

Do not feel guilty! Why should you feel guilty for doing what is right?

5 MEEKNESS VS FACTIONS

INSPIRATION....MEEKNESS

Once upon a time, there was a Prince who fell desperately in love with a peasant girl in a nearby village. The Prince had professed his love for her repeatedly but still felt that he had not expressed his love adequately. His thoughts were, "How can I show her how much I love her in a very tangible way?"

After much thought, he decided that he would give her an amazing stallion of which he was very proud. This raging black stallion was massive, and he pranced in a manner of elegance that illuminated his power and majestic nature. Without question, that powerful beast commanded awe in the eye of anyone who saw him. His presence was very imposing.

When the Prince brought the horse to the young peasant girl, she was very fearful of such a huge enormous animal. She asked of the Prince, "I am but a small peasant girl. Why, oh Prince, would you offer me such a huge, raging stallion?" The Prince replied with pride, "This is the meekest horse that I possess. Although he possesses great strength and character, he responds to only a gentle nudge of his bridle. He requires no bit in his mouth to have him respond to his master's touch. He can be guided with only a gentle nudge without resistance. He is one with his master. He has his *power under control*."

31

"Power under control" is the very definition of meekness. As an inspired individual, we, like this raging stallion, should be acutely aware of the spiritual strength at our disposal through the power of the Holy Spirit.

Just as this raging stallion responds to the gentle nudge of his master's direction, so we should yield to the gentle nudge of the Holy Spirit when faced with choices and motivational stimuli.

An interesting point the Prince makes to his love is that no "bit" is required in the horse's mouth to make him respond to his master. For those who do not have an equine background, the bit is a tack device, generally made of metal that is added to a bridle and is placed behind the horse's teeth to *force* the horse to respond to the directions of the horseman. The bit enables a source of communication with the horse as it exerts pressure in the horse's mouth. The bit is not comfortable, but very necessary to have control over the animal.

The fact that no bit is required in the mouth of the Prince's horse illuminates the fact the horse and rider has a very close relationship and responds to the gentle moves that the master instructs. Our Master is the most powerful source in the universe, and if we easily yield to His direction, we will follow His path of *inspiration* with a mere nudge; no pressure will be required. We will not be *forced* to respond, but very *willing*.

How rewarding it will be when we fully realize that to be *meek* is not an indication of weakness or impotence in our lives. There is no need to cower down to man or circumstance. We can walk upright with complete assurance that what resides within us is the very power that created our universe. We have a divine source of "power steering" that can handle most rugged terrain that we could ever encounter.

Where He leads, we will follow!

"May the God of hope fill you with all joy and peace as you trust in him,
so that you may overflow with hope by the power of the Holy Spirit."
(Romans 15:13)

M OTIVATION....FACTIONS

Let's go back and revisit the HotShot Motor Company for a moment. If you will remember, the very first thing that happened after the sales meeting was the development of several factions within the sales staff; the old experienced guys, the single Moms, the baseball haters, the complainers, the new guy, and all the others. This staff became at odds with the owner's incentive plan causing them to splinter into separate smaller groups of complainers, which, in turn, caused them to be at odds with each other. They fragmented. They lost their potential for synergy. Their synergistic potential broke down at the last word of the motivated incentive plan. With this type of fragmentation, Mr. Ross' incentive plan didn't have a leg to stand on.

When the term "synergy" arises, my first thought is the tackling sled on my high school football field. That sled provides a great demonstration of the power of synergy.

A tackling sled has one function; to prove to a group of players how important it is to work together, moving in the same direction. Granted the strength that one garners from conquering the resistance is physically beneficial, but there is a bigger picture. Let's take a look.

Each of the six players lines up and individually runs as hard as possible and digs his shoulder into the pad on the tackling sled. For simplicity purposes, let's say that each player moves the sled forward a distance of ten inches. So, if all six hit it together they will move the sled sixty inches, right? WRONG!! Those six players can move the sled all the way down the field, out of the gate, and down Main Street! Why? SYNERGY!

Synergy is the dynamic of overcoming resistance collectively with a less proportionate amount of energy. Each of the players actually used a smaller amount of energy to accomplish a much greater purpose. They were all moving in the same direction with a common goal in mind.
The problem with the HotShot Motor Company incentive plan was that it blew up immediately due to the factions it created. The plan lacked any synergy at all. For a group of individuals to move in the same direction there must be a common mindset, striving toward a common goal, where everyone benefits from the effort.

33

The incentive plan fragmented by sending everyone in various and opposing directions losing any chance of the collective synergy the dealer thought that would occur. Fragmentation happens any time there is only one winner.

Any collective group of people; be it a company, a church, a family, or even a just a couple, can overcome the source of resistance when they push together, in the same direction, with a common goal, and with less expended energy. TEAMWORK!

Remember the cowboy movies? Most of the stage coaches would have a team of horses numbering four or six horses. Those horses were able to travel over so many miles because each horse was using less energy to pull the stagecoach. The goal wasn't to have just enough horses to pull the weight, but have enough horses to go the distance.

At an equestrian event, you can witness the ultimate expression of synergy when you watch the trick riders as they stand to ride on the backs of a pair of horses that have been trained to be in perfect sync with each other at every move. The rider depends on their *synergy* for his or her safety. It is a beautiful effort to witness.

Motivating individuals have no regard for synergy because it defeats their purpose. They actually enjoy the resistance and fragmentation. If they can dispel the forward movement of others, it will facilitate their agenda. If the larger volume of a group can be fragmented into factions, their agenda appears to have less resistance to encounter; less competition for a motivator. A motivator's agenda is always to promote SELF.

"I urge you, brothers and sisters, to watch out for those
*who **cause** divisions and put obstacles in your way that are*
contrary to the teaching you have learned. Keep away from them."
(Romans 16:17)

Be watchful of those that cause divisions and create chaos among others. They are the gossipers, the fatalists, the agitators, the contentious and argumentative individuals whose focus is only on the negative aspects. Being *watchful* is not *judgment* but *discernment*.

Be careful, because, with time, you WILL become their target. Book it!

Here are a few phrases that will tip you off every time:

"Now, don't say anything but...."
"If I were running this company/church...."
"Guess what I just heard...."
"Don't repeat this but...."
"Now, I didn't say this but...."

These statements are generally an attempt to have you "triangulate" against someone, some entity, or some ideal. *Triangulation* draws you into an unwitting alliance with the motivator. You will become part of the problem when you had no intent just be anything but an innocent bystander. You may have no interest in the situation at all. If this happens, the motivator will use your name as an ally to his or her cause.

"Furthermore, just as they did not think it worthwhile to retain the knowledge of God, so God gave them over to a depraved mind so that they do what ought not to be done. They have become filled with every kind of wickedness, evil, greed, and depravity. They are full of envy, murder, strife, deceit, and malice. They are gossipers, slanderers, God-haters, insolent, arrogant and boastful; they invent ways of doing evil; they disobey their parent. They have no understanding, no fidelity, no love, and no mercy."
(Romans 1:28-31)

6 LOVE VS HATRED

INSPIRATION.... LOVE

When we read the Biblical list of the Fruit Of The Spirit, the second fruit is "Love." I hope that you will indulge me for disrupting that order by placing the subject of love in this position of our contrasting points. I wanted this discussion to be at the heart of the journey we are taking together. I also wanted to place it following the scripture that appeared at the end of the last chapter. One line so aptly describes the intent and heart of the motivator; "they have no understanding, no fidelity, no love, no mercy...." No love! Chilling!

I honestly cannot think of a word that has been more misused and maligned than the word "love." To love *someone* and to love some *thing* is an entirely different dynamic. Sadly, history has proven time after time that these two dynamics have, in the mind and hearts of many, become synonymous when, in all actuality, they are also polar opposites just like *Inspiration and Motivation.*

I must confess that I love British Leyland sports cars. I would love to have another Triumph TR-6 like the one I owned back in the '70s; light canary yellow, wire wheels, A-Barth exhaust system, electric overdrive, with both a black convertible top and a black bolt-on hardtop. A beauty! But...

Sadly, the day came when it was just not suitable for a "family" car, so I had to trade it for something with more room and protection. Was it responsible? Yes. Was it reprehensible? You bet! I loved that car! I took such good care of it. I could actually repair it myself. There were no computers! I could change the brakes and tune those twin Stromberg carburetors to perfection. It was my baby! But...

Another "baby "came along; a pretty little blue-eyed girl who gave me the opportunity to learn to express an entirely different kind of love. That love was not expendable or saleable. I might have "loved" the TR-6 to the max, but that car could easily be traded for another, but I wouldn't have traded that little girl for anything in the world.

The kind of love I felt for that little girl was totally *inspired*. That love came from within my heart, and my ultimate goal was to give her the greatest of care possible and be able to fix whatever problems that might come along. The Spirit within me would give me guidance enabling me to meet those goals.

Oh sure, I loved that TR-6, but it was merely a matter of mechanical lust. I was not *inspired* to love that car. I was *motivated* by the styling and excitement it provided me as I took the top down and headed to the Blue Ridge Parkway for an afternoon ride. It was exhilarating!

What was the difference? Quite simply, it was a *relationship*. A child has an innate nature to give their love to you without conditions. God gives us the opportunity to try to build a child's nature and character from the ground up. With diligent care and divine guidance, we can hopefully craft the worldview of a child that would hopefully glorify God. When a child has problems, we can depend on a divine mechanic who can work wonders through the power of His Spirit.

A child doesn't roll off an assembly line where many hands have constructed the parts in an efficient manner to ensure that it works properly and meets the public eye with applause. A child, fearfully and wonderfully made, teaches us love, joy, patience, empathy, sympathy, trust, gentleness, kindness, meekness, and self-control.

On a day to day basis, we may not experience overt expressions of love from our employment circle or from the customers we serve, or even our family, but every moment of every day does afford us the opportunity express a lifestyle of *inspiration* to those we deal with regardless of how *motivating* they become.

Behind the walls of the front showroom at the HotShot Motor Company finds a beehive of activity....the Service Department. Bill is the Service Manager. Every day Bill is highly *motivated* by customer complaints due to failures in automotive systems that he had nothing to do with the implementation of the parts or design. But who receives the brunt of the customer disdain? Bill does!! Regardless of the fact that he is standing there ready to help in any way possible, no effort ever seems to be good enough. He is the victim of motivation on every side.

Think about this for a moment. Have you ever rolled into the service lane and jumped out of your car and ran to the service desk to tell them what a great car you are driving and what a great job they are doing.? Of course not! But, if one small, minute, petty problem persists on someone's car or truck, Bill will be crucified on the Customer Service Rating portion of the dealer's website. He didn't build the vehicle. The factory did! He had no input in the design. The new model "updates" were as big of a surprise to him as they were to anyone else, and the new tools to handle the updates are back ordered for six weeks. Bill can't win for losing! *Motivated* to the max due to things that are, in no way, under his control.

Now, just how *inspired* would you be if you were to awake every morning knowing that Bill's job awaited your arrival? His job is to deal with constant *motivation*. Oh, it doesn't stop with the customer base. Internally, the Sales Department and the Parts Department constantly try to pick the pockets of his profits by continually asking favors on services that cost him his departmental profits every time.

Bill is truly between a rock and a hard place! What can he do? It doesn't appear that he is able to satisfy anyone. He can only do one thing....

Operate under the inspirational and not allow the motivational circumstances to affect him. His most effective coping method is to honor God with choices that will glorify Him in everything that he says, thinks, or does. Can Bill be condemned for his actions? No! "Against these things, there is no law." If Bill is condemned for his inspirational actions or lifestyle, it will be quite apparent who the real *motivators* are in his world. Living a life of *inspiration* will always expose your *dissenters*. They will rear their ugly heads and produce the fruit of the flesh every time.

"But I tell you, love your enemies and pray for those who persecute you."
(Matthew5:44)

"Love is patient; love is kind. It does not envy; it does not boast, it is not proud."
(1Corinthians13:4)

"A new command I give you: Love one another. As I have loved you, so you must love one another. By this everyone will know that you are my disciples if you love one another."
(John13:34-35)

"Be   devoted   to one another in love.   Honor one   another above yourselves."
(Romans 12:10)

"Treat your neighbors as yourself… but don't take down the fence."
– Carl Sandburg

MOTIVATION.... HATRED

Wow! The word "hatred" is so strong! It cuts like a knife. Are there actually people in my circle of influence that really do hate intensely? Absolutely! Bank on it!

Their hatred may not be directed at you personally, but they may hate what you think, say, or do. They may hate the fact that you are at peace. They may hate what or who you stand for. They may hate the fact that people gravitate to you for no apparent reason. They may hate the fact that no one comes to them for guidance or counsel. They may hate the fact that, for some odd reason, they cannot *motivate* you to satisfy their agenda. They may hate the fact that they hate so much that they are hated. They may hate the fact that their actions have caused them tremendous isolation. That may hate the fact that their hate is not more productive, but diminished and dismissed, by those who are *inspired*.

There just might be some members of your family that don't hate you personally but do hate all of the same items above as they are demonstrated in your personal life. They are miserable! You don't need to be! You are not called to be a motivator's doormat.

There may be some folks in your church that operate exactly the same way. "Oh no, that can't happen in MY church!" Oh no? Well, just try deciding what color of carpet to put in the new building! Then step back and watch the flesh flash! Whooee!! Hey! There's a brand new church in town! Church split!! It happens all the time.

"If this kind of hatred exists in my circle of family and friends, what do I do to fix it?" The answer is very simple.... Nothing! It is not your problem. It is their problem to resolve. It is incumbent upon them to take action to correct the *motivational* behavior. The best course of action will always be to remain silent. Don't throw fuel on their fire.

Albert Einstein said, "Weak people revenge. Strong people forgive. Intelligent people ignore."

Do you want to conquer motivational actions that solicit a response? Here is a list of responses and coping skills that will diffuse the actions.

Realize that you do not have to understand the "why."
Realize that it is not your problem but theirs
Solving their circumstance is not in your job description
The many do not have to suffer for the few
Get out of God's way
Do not cause confusion
Do not try to convince
Allow the Spirit to convict
Continue to embrace the Fruit Of The Spirit
Do not abandon your lifestyle of Inspiration
Continue to glorify God in all you think, do, and say
There is only one Savior and it ain't you!
Be still and know that He is God!
Let God do it!

Enabling a *motivator* is not going to resolve any of their conflicts. They must be allowed to hit the wall, and finally understand that serious corrections are desperately needed in their life if they are going to ever live in peace with others and with themselves.

I have heard this statement so many times, "Oh that's just the way he (or she) IS." No! ... It is the way they have been *allowed* to be; endorsed and sponsored by their enabler. An enabler will never allow their victims the opportunity to account for their own responsibilities. The victim!

An *enabler* is the highest form of a *motivator,* and the monsters they create are known as narcissists and sociopaths; the ultimate in the species of the self- centered.

7 KINDNESS VS SELFISH AMBITION

INSPIRATION.... KINDNESS

Back at the HotShot Motor Company, a very special meeting is about to take place. Mr. Ross, the dealer, has asked the sales manager to send Brad into his office. They need to talk... (Uh - Oh!)

Brad has been with the company for around seven years. He has never been the Super Hero Sales Award (SHSA) winner, but he is steadily in the top ten producers and rarely misses a day of work. He is a team player and very consistent. Brad isn't an overly aggressive individual, but keeps a steady pace and is great with his customers. They all love and trust him. His phone calls are always welcome, and no one ducks out of sight from him at the grocery store. In fact, they seem actually to seek him out. His referral volume is outstanding. His customers depend on him. He diffuses their fears. He's just a great guy and professional.

Brad knocks on the dealer's door and is asked in. The dealer doesn't even rise to greet him, no handshake, but sits in his large judge's chair that is positioned behind his enormous desk. He is looking out of the window. Plaques litter the walls as well as many pictures of Mr. Ross with notable individuals and sports figures. The indirect lighting makes for a very comfortable office atmosphere. Mr. Ross, without even turning around in his chair to face Brad begins to speak. Then, with commanding drama, Mr. Ross slowly turns toward Brad...

43

"Brad, I have had you on my mind quite a bit lately. I asked to meet with you today to discuss your production and your attitude." At this statement, Brad begins to wonder what in the world he might be referring to; Production? Attitude? What could possibly be wrong?

"Brad, I've watched you with your customers and quite frankly...
You are TOO nice! You could be the top salesman on the board, but you are going to have to toughen up and get control of your customers. Stop believing every word they say and push early for a close. Don't let them lead you around the lot from car to car. In fact, don't even show them a car until you have asked them if they are ready to buy a car T-O-D-A-Y!! You are just wasting your time. You've gotta get control! If they start talking about anything but a car purchase, change the subject back to the sale! You don't need to know their family business. Just sell a car! Where they attend church doesn't mean anything! You should not be concerned in what activities their kids participate. Just sell the car! That is the reason you are here! You are here to make money. Just sell the car! Don't make friends! Make sales!

Brad is somewhat taken aback by Mr. Ross's remarks. Every "after sale survey" returns giving him glowing remarks. Every customer said that they would gladly recommend him to their family and friends, and they would happily be back to buy another car from him as long as he is employed at the HotShot Motor Company. Brad knows that he treats every customer with ultimate respect and honors their requests for truthful information. He gives them factual information and does not over-promise or under-deliver. He is filled with product knowledge and never operates outside of his job description but ...Brad is just TOO nice.

Brad, although not even invited to sit down, does so anyway. He leans back in the leather office chair appearing completely relaxed and crosses his leg, which renders the dealer rather uneasy. Mr. Ross felt certain that he would motivate him with his admonishment. Brad's body language doesn't indicate that he is bothered in the least. Ross' admonition hasn't had any effect on Brad at all.

"Mr. Ross, I appreciate your compliment that I am "TOO nice" to my customers out on the lot. I would hope that I am always perceived to be just that...."TOO nice", because that is exactly what my Mama would expect me to be. She taught me well, and I hope that I honor her every day through my care and concern for others, including you sir.

He continues, "I am not sure, but I am certain you must have noticed that my "repeat-purchase percentage" is higher than anyone else on the sales staff. My repossession rate is virtually zero. I always leave some headroom for the finance manager to offer product sales, and my customers buy more extended warranties than any other salesperson in the dealership. My factory delivery process scores are the highest in the entire dealership. But, I'm sure you are aware of that." He continues...

"I probably didn't even need to mention any of those things to you because I am sure you have observed those items and how they have added to your bottom-line over last several years. I believe that my being "TOO nice" must have had something to do with those stellar scores, percentages, and my capacity to create additional income on each of one my sales impacting your bottom line."

Mr. Ross wasn't even remotely aware of these supportive sales percentages which always translate greatly into dollars for the bottom line and in Brad's case; quite steadily. Mr. Ross thought for a moment.

"Well Brad, I just want you to be number one! I want you to be a winner! You could be a manager one day!" Brad replied with a smile on his face, "Mr. Ross, the only person who can cause me to become number one on the board is ME. If becoming number one requires me to compromise who I am with my customers, I can't help but believe that I would then actually be failing; my customers and myself. If it's all right with you, I'll just continue to be...TOO nice. Is that okay?" Brad thanked him and walked out of the dealer's office without a response. (Good close Brad!) Mr. Ross turns back to the window staring in thought. "Your Mama!"

I know that I would certainly want a salesperson like Brad. If being number one meant anything to Brad, he would attain it, but not at the sacrifice of his personality, character, or credibility. Brad IS #1!

Let's take a moment and revisit your personal inventory. How are you perceived by your peers or clients? No matter what the environment, there is no valid reason to be anything but "TOO nice" to the people you encounter daily. Being nice is probably what your Mama taught you too. Mind your Mama!

M OTIVATION....SELFISH AMBITION

Probably no more obvious of an indicator of *motivation* is the actions of an individual who is consumed with *selfish ambition*. Nothing is sacred to them. A Selfishly Ambitious Person (SAP) has no regard for anything or anyone other than themselves. No matter what relationship structure is in place; business, church, team sports, or even the family, they operate solely to satisfy their own desires to benefit and exalt themselves. Top dogs are living high on the hog!

These individuals are the ultimate as motivators. SAPs respond to outside empty motivation quicker than anyone. They will try their best to utilize your gifts and talents to lift them to the higher plane that they envision. It amazes me at how aggressive these individuals can be.

The paradox is, that after doing whatever damage was required in the wake to elevate him or herself they always become the tragic victim when they begin to fail. The failing situation at hand is ALWAYS the fault of everyone else. Heaven forbid that they reap what they have sown! And why do they have no support from those around them? No one cares about me! (Wah! Wah!) Isn't that just so pitiful? NO! It is pathetic!

Quite simply, a SAP is a bully. A SAP will climb over anyone to attain their goals; real or imagined. What is remarkable is how these bullies will clamor to get whatever they fancy regardless of its true value. They just want to win or be in the limelight. A SAP has to be number one!

On occasion during a sales meeting at HotShot Motor Company, Mr. Ross will have bills of various denominations (not the Baptist or Methodist kind) wadded up in his pocket; several one dollar bills, a couple of fives, a couple of tens, a couple of twenties, and a sole one hundred dollar bill. At a moment of "surprise," he will throw them high

46

in the air and watch the salespeople scramble to retrieve them. They will jump, climb, fall, and tumble all over each other just to grab one or more of those flying bills. Eddie won't be participating for the next while though. He is still nursing that broken arm he received getting to that one dollar bill the last time. *Motivated!* Oh, the cost of motivation!

Their "Golden Rule" for a SAP is "Do unto others BEFORE they do unto you." The deluded part of that mantra is that the SAP believes that everyone else thinks likes he or she thinks, which makes a SAP very paranoid. A SAP thinks everyone wants to treat him the way that he treats people. There is always someone out to get them. "Everybody is against me." No, a SAP is against everyone else. How deluded is a SAP when they believe that others want to be just like they are. WRONG!

There are a few SAPs at HotShot Motors; the worst is Gerald. It seems Gerald is first on the board just about every month. Gerald will promise a customer anything to get them to agree to buy a car. He rarely tells the truth. He will promise any payment needed to close the customer. He does "whatever it takes"...except, actually SELL the car. Gerald knows that if he can just get the customer to commit to buying, he can flip the deal to the finance manager and he will close the deal for him because, after all, the finance manager is the "closer." Gerald will use the finance manager's closing ability to "sell" the car. And, if for some reason the finance manager can't close the deal due to Gerald's deception and inept procedures, the loss of that customer will certainly not be Gerald's fault. Gerald will state the finance manager just "blew" his customer out. "What a weak closer!" ... in Gerald's mind anyway.

Gerald wants everyone else to do the homework while he gets the grade. Oh, I am sure that you have encountered people in every strata of life that have this same mindset. You do the work, and they will be glad to take the grade or get the credit without earning it.

There is nothing wrong with ambition at all, but when it becomes *selfish ambition*, that is another story. True ambition only costs the *ambitious* his or her efforts. *Selfish ambition* costs everyone else BUT the SAP their efforts.

SAPs exist in just about every organizational structure known to man. Someone is constantly trying to elevate themselves to gain whatever they deem important; money, status, accolades, public approval, control, and a myriad of other scenarios. There is never enough.

SAPs also exhibit some personality traits that are sure-fire indicators of who and what they are; arrogant, haughty, condemning, entitled, judgmental, cocky, superiority, scheming, and braggadocios.

To a SAP, you are the fuel and the fire. You are to be consumed!

"Pride goes before destruction, a haughty spirit before a fall."
(Proverbs 16:18)

"There are six things the LORD hates, seven that are detestable to Him: haughty eyes, a lying tongue, hands that shed innocent blood, a heart that devises wicked schemes, feet that are quick to rush into evil."
(Proverbs 6:16-18)

8 GOODNESS VS FITS OF RAGE

INSPIRATION....GOODNESS

When the Corn family moved to the Smoky Mountains in 1994, our daughters were very young and started elementary school in a wonderful school on the outskirts of town. Having moved from the "big city" of Nashville/Hendersonville, our girls went to school a bit more well dressed than some of the local kids here in the mountains.

Keep in mind that their environment had been a bit more cosmopolitan and in their home, the major points of our conversations were spiritual in nature. Our home was, and forever shall be, Christ-centered.

One particular day, shortly after our move here, our eldest became the brunt of the wrath of some vicious little mountain girls. They called her foul names and swore at her. She didn't respond. She didn't know how to respond like that. She had never experienced that section of the vocabulary before. She had never experienced even that kind of behavior before. She was stunned, silent, shocked, and out of her element. As she stared silently at the girls, one of the girls angrily chided her, "Are you too good to say something like that to us?"

Her response was priceless, "No I'm not... but one day I am going to stand before the Lord, and He's going to tell me all the things I said and did to other people... and I don't want Him to keep me very long."

Those girls never bothered her again and actually, in time, became her good friends. She later discovered that the father of one of the girls was in prison and her mother a drug addict. In addition to all of that to bear, her uncle was sexually abusing her. Gee? I can't imagine why that child was so angry at that pristine little new girl from the Christ-centered home? She was a victim of a very rough family environment.

Obviously, that child had not been exposed to very much *goodness* in her life. Her life, at such a young age, was consumed with *motivating* circumstances. Life for her was a life of terror compared to our daughter's life. No wonder she wanted to lash out. That is exactly what happens when people have no *goodness* in their lives, they lash out and become bitter. Misery does love company, and they will *motivate* you to join them.

Goodness is not a matter of just being behaviorally good. Experiencing the goodness of others around you is of great importance to a child. They "need" goodness to flow into their lives. They want desperately to experience the goodness of others. They are hurting and "hurting people hurt people." It is a given. It should be no surprise that someone who has never received goodness in their life would not have the capacity to give goodness to others. Except...

If the Spirit of God resides within you, regardless of your personal history, goodness can pour forth through you to others like a river through the power of the Holy Spirit. You may not think you have the *capability*, but I can assure you that when you have the right Spirit within, you will not only have the *capability* but the *capacity* as well. You will draw people to you like a well in the desert.

> " Our God specializes in good things.
> Things that you and I really need.
> Good things for the body and spirit.
> All you have to do is just believe"
> ("Good Things" – The Hemphills 1981)

Inspiring others is rarely a problem when you are filled with *goodness*. Your heart's desires will be filled with the goodness that the Spirit gives you to share. When you experience persecution by others for your goodness, you will not have to back down. Goodness always prevails.

"Give me a sign of your goodness, that my enemies may see it and be put to shame, for you, LORD, have helped me and comforted me."
(Psalm 86:17)

"..make every effort to add to your faith goodness; and to goodness, knowledge; and to knowledge, self-control; and to self-control, perseverance; and to perseverance, godliness."
(2 Peter 1:5-6)

M OTIVATION.... FITS OF RAGE

What a stark contrast between these two items; Goodness and Fits Of Rage! One could only hope that they would not be the brunt of someone's fits of rage but, as you read previously, even a young child can be the target of someone's fits of rage. It frequently happens; road rage, school shootings, fighting at ballgames, bullying, and various forms of intimidation, and abuse in the home and workplace.

In the news today we are very likely to hear a story daily of some form of "abuse"; spousal, child, spiritual, physical, mental, elder, or sexual abuse. All of these abuses have a similar root to their problem; *Unresolved anger.*

Motivators tend to have short fuses. They demand that their desires are met immediately, or their wrath will quickly ensue. Motivators hold the world around them as hostages, and no ransom is ever enough to satisfy them.

Motivators will always cry out... "Me first!"

I can't imagine that anyone in today's society is not familiar with the term PTSD; Post Traumatic Stress Disorder. PTSD is most commonly associated with military personnel as a result of the heinous experiences a soldier endures in the throes of a conflict. Do not discount or minimize the disorder. It is real and has profound effects.

PTSD is considered a result of war experiences. It is a condition that results from doing their job. However, there are many other forms of PTSD that are the results of traumatic experiences endured by adults and children such as family discord, a divorce, fires, loss of their home, or the sudden death of a parent or loved one. These are just a few examples.

There is another PTSD scenario that takes a major toll on adults and children; perpetual physical or mental abuse over a prolonged period of time by someone who is a family, spiritual, or some type of an authority figure; C-PTSD/Complex Post Traumatic Stress Disorder.

C-PTSD encompasses many dysfunctions that are not at all war-related. One common thread through the various areas of conflict is being held, *hostage*. A kidnap victim may spend years as a hostage to someone who systematically abuses them in various ways. This end result of the ordeal is horrifying! We have all heard stories over the years where young girls and boys have been subjected to this very horrifying experience creating highly *motivated* individuals. They become dysfunctional to the point of embracing their abusers. It is their "normal".

A hostage situation doesn't have to be a dramatic abduction. A child or an adult might be a hostage in their very own home. They may be held hostage emotionally by a dismissive or abusive father, mother, or sibling. There is a trickle-down effect in most of these scenarios; the parents are likely treating their child the very way he or she was treated in the past by their father or mother. Parents that were constantly angry and combative become the standard of behavior for the child. Again, it then becomes their perspective of "normal."

A spouse may be held hostage to the non-redemptive habits, abuses, or dysfunctions of their spouse. In time, the anger builds and becomes more and more explosive. This type of perpetual stress causes the abused to feel less and less of a human, diminishing their self-worth and self-image. Eventually, the abused will cower down or eventually, violently fight back. One way or another, the rage is there inside of them and, at some point, something will trigger a fit of rage.

As a parent, I am acutely aware that a child, even with the most favorable environment and upbringing, can become a huge source of contention and disappointment. You can scratch your scalp bloody wondering, "Was this child switched at birth? Surely he or she belongs to someone else!" Welcome to parenthood! If you allow the child to rule the home, you can be held hostage to the child's personality, tantrums, delusions, emotional blackmail, lies, and general lack of respect. It is time for some serious intervention… the Holy Spirit! A direct hit from God appears to be the only solution! Only the conviction of the Holy Spirit will turn the tide. Surrender in only one way…to God.

"Held hostage"… That phrase leads us to believe that there is no escape. But, I can assure you that there is! Through any and all *motivational* scenarios *Inspiration* always conquers *Motivation* and with no collateral damage.

Instead of expecting a dramatic change in the Motivator, simply operate inside the parameters of *Inspiration*, which affords you the opportunity to enjoy the peace and joy that is available to you. You must learn that you do not have to accept the invitation to participate in every argument that you are invited to. The solution is as simple as making a good choice; a choice that follows the leading of the Spirit within you. Do not take the bait! You don't have to justify *inspiration*. Do not RSVP!

Now I am about to offer you a simple fact that just might offend you or, at least, deflate your super-spiritual ego;

"There is only one Savior…and it ain't you!"

If *Inspiration* is to overcome *Motivation,* you must realize your limits. Do as you are inspired and then… Let go! Get out of God's way! The Spirit's *conviction* will always trump your *convincing*… EVERY TIME!

"Rudeness is a weak person's imitation of strength"

"Hurting people hurt people"

Held hostage? By man or circumstance? You can be free from the wrath of others by simply not responding. Just turn and walk away.

Proverbs 15

A gentle answer turns away wrath,

but a harsh word stirs up anger.

The tongue of the wise adorns knowledge,

but the mouth of the fool gushes folly.

The eyes of the LORD are everywhere,

keeping watch on the wicked and the good.

The soothing tongue is a tree of life,

but a perverse tongue crushes the spirit.

A fool spurns a parent's discipline,

but whoever heeds correction shows prudence.

The house of the righteous contains great treasure,

but the income of the wicked brings ruin.

The lips of the wise spread knowledge,

but the hearts of fools are not upright.

The LORD detests the sacrifice of the wicked,

but the prayer of the upright pleases him.

The LORD detests the way of the wicked,

but he loves those who pursue righteousness.

Stern discipline awaits anyone who leaves the path;

the one who hates correction will die.

Death and Destruction[a] lie open before the LORD—

how much more do human hearts!

Mockers resent correction,

so they avoid the wise.

A happy heart makes the face cheerful,

but heartache crushes the spirit.

The discerning heart seeks knowledge,

but the mouth of a fool feeds on folly.

All the days of the oppressed are wretched,

but the cheerful heart has a continual feast.

Better a little with the fear of the LORD

than great wealth with turmoil.

Better a small serving of vegetables with love

than a fattened calf with hatred.

A hot-tempered person stirs up conflict,

but the one who is patient calms a quarrel.

The way of the sluggard is blocked with thorns,

but the path of the upright is a highway.

A wise son brings joy to his father,

but a foolish man despises his mother.

Folly brings joy to one who has no sense,

but whoever has understanding keeps a straight course.

Plans fail for lack of counsel,

but with many advisers, they succeed.

A person finds joy in giving an apt reply—

and how good is a timely word!

The path of life leads upward for the prudent

to keep them from going down to the realm of the dead.

The LORD tears down the house of the proud,

but he sets the widow's boundary stones in place.

The LORD detests the thoughts of the wicked,

but gracious words are pure in his sight.

The greedy bring ruin to their households,

but the one who hates bribes will live.

The heart of the righteous weighs its answers,
but the mouth of the wicked gushes evil.
The LORD is far from the wicked,
but he hears the prayer of the righteous.
Light in a messenger's eyes brings joy to the heart,
and good news gives health to the bones.
Whoever heeds life-giving correction
will be at home among the wise.
Those who disregard discipline despise themselves,
but the one who heeds correction gains understanding.
Wisdom's instruction is to fear the LORD,
and humility comes before honor.

9 PATIENCE VS ADDICTIONS

INSPIRATION.... PATIENCE

In the realm of patience, my least favorite question that I might be asked is, "Would you mind if I put you on hold for a few seconds?" Mentally I am saying, "Oh yeah! Right! Like I am going to tell you that I really do mind and how being on hold irritates me to no end? I hope I don't have a birthday before someone finally comes back on the line!"

Oops! I suppose I'd better get it together and not *react* in such a way internally. Gotta remember, "10% of what happens to me... 90% of how I react to it" so, I politely in my sweet Southern way, "No problem."

Being "on hold" is not my favorite place to be, but it sure does beat losing the opportunity to speak to real, live, human being about my problems or concerns. After all, I could get one of those robots asking me to leave my number for a call back as soon as an agent gets free. I will not *lose my place in line*. Really? How do I know I won't lose my place in line? The only salvation there could be in that situation would be that my eardrums aren't assaulted with static-laden distorted music that repeatedly plays in the "on hold" loop. That music is highly motivational! It gives me shivers!

If being on hold is the worst thing that happens to me on any given day, I have it made! It has been said many times that "Patience is a virtue."

In the microwave society we live in today, it appears that every circumstance demands immediate attention. Many bad choices are made due to our lack of patience. Just how virtuous are we when we make bad choices? Most folks have no patience at all, yet they claim to be filled with the Holy Spirit. "Give me patience Lord!" Hey! You already have it!

NEWS FLASH!! If you are filled with the Holy Spirit, you already have the gift of patience. Patience is part of the Fruit Of The Spirit that you possess. You have it whether you realize it or not. You just have to exercise it. Just like a muscle, for it to be effective, it must be exercised.

No one likes to wait, but "waiting on the Lord" is imperative if you are to make the right choices that vanquish motivational circumstances.

"Be still, and know that I am God; I will be exalted among the nations, I will be exalted in the earth."
                    (Psalm 46:10)

Our patience in waiting on the Lord will exalt Him here on earth. Those around us will witness His peace and our faith, as we trust Him to handle our situations to a conclusion that glorifies Him. Patience is an extension of faith and trust. We know that God CAN do (Faith). Patience tells the world that God WILL do (Trust).

Patience is often confused with "tolerance." Having tolerance enables us to *endure* motivating circumstances. Patience calls upon us to *overcome* those circumstances with *inspiration*. Enduring doesn't call for resolution through our Spirit. *Enduring* calls us to continue to deal with the motivating circumstances on a continuing basis. This is actually the essence of being *motivated*.

Here is a perfect example of the difference between patience and tolerance from a resident in the Great Smoky Mountains.....Me!
In The Great Smoky Mountains area, we have twelve and a half million visitors yearly that come to enjoy the National Park, the scenery, and

the family-oriented activities that our area affords them. Needless to say, the traffic is a complete pain very often. It is "intolerable."

I live in Sevierville, TN and I could have a function in Pigeon Forge, TN which is just a couple of miles away. During the summer season, I would be foolish to try to go from Sevierville to Pigeon Forge on the Parkway. Without question, I would never be able to gauge the time it would take me to get to my function because of the bumper-to-bumper traffic. Now, my being a "local," I am acutely aware of the back roads that will drop me off at various points in Pigeon Forge while bypassing the onslaught of traffic on the Parkway. Sitting on the Parkway in the heat of the summer does not test my *patience*. It challenges my *tolerance*! BIG TIME!

With patience, the Lord will be glorified. I can assure you that if you have a function to attend at a specific time, and you are stuck on the Parkway...you WILL NOT glorify God!

Be assured that someone will want to change lanes creating a major traffic jam as they try to cross not one, but two lanes of traffic to get to their destination at Burger King. Intolerable! And to the guy who runs out of gas and stalls the entire forward progression, "Buy gas!! You just passed seven gas stations in the last two miles!" See! I told you! God isn't glorified! Intolerable! (Tip-off: Exclamation points!)

When we are patient, we will be at peace. We will accomplish our tasks as we should while trusting Him to bring our situation to a glorifying resolve.

"Therefore, as God's chosen people, holy and dearly loved, clothe yourselves with compassion, kindness, humility, gentleness, and patience."
(Colossians 3:12)

"The end of a matter is better than its beginning, and patience is better than pride."
(Ecclesiastes 7:8)

MOTIVATION.... ADDICTIONS

Addictions... Yikes! That is one scary word! When we hear that word, our minds are generally directed to the most common, front page addictions that we regularly hear: drugs, alcohol, porn, sex, eating, and gambling.

Billions of dollars are spent yearly by individuals to support their habits. Addictions destroy. They destroy lives, families, and fortunes. When have you ever heard of any addiction that glorified God? Never!

In our day to day lives, we are with addicts much more frequently than we might think. "What? I don't associate with drug addicts, alcoholics, or gamblers!" Might you say? You may be surprised to know that there are addicts all around you and you haven't a clue. Let's define addiction.

"Addiction is a condition that results when a person ingests a substance (for example, alcohol, cocaine, nicotine) or engages in an activity (such as gambling, sex, shopping) that can be pleasurable, but the continuation of which becomes compulsive and *interferes with ordinary responsibilities and concerns, such as work, ...*"
(Psychology Today)

That is a very compelling definition, but I have another ...

"Addiction is a choice motivated by man or circumstance."

Everything that we do, think or say comes down to a *choice*. There is no escaping the fact that every choice we make has consequences. God's gift of *Free Will* does not grant us *Free Reign* without consequences.

Every addiction comes with two components that are extremely powerful; false gratification and bondage. It is very easy to accept that statement when it relates to sex, drugs, or alcohol. The chance of our having known someone that has fallen prey to one of these "substances" is probably not at all remote. The consequences have surely been hideous. But....

Let's revisit the above definition of addiction for a moment. Notice the last few words, "but the continuation of which becomes *compulsive* and *interferes with ordinary responsibilities and concerns, such as work.*"

There are so many other things that can be addictive that will promote false gratification and bondage. These are costly and can become very divisive in family and friendships, create hatred and discord, foster fits of rage, selfishness, cause mental abandonment as to responsibility, and alienate others.

Sports
Music
Hobbies
Automotive Activities
Internet
Video Games
Television
Shopping
Binge Eating
Smoking
Attention
Social Media
Church
Ministry

Ah Ha! Now you realize how many addicted people you may actually know! The above list is but a small portion of the things that people have embraced deep obsessions that they must contend with. Each one could be dissected to show how they are truly *motivational* and *all-consuming*.

A keyword that is commonly used for addictions is a *compulsion*. If we have an activity in our lives that is a *compulsion*, then we are steeped in *motivation*. A compulsive act is born from our being *compelled* to do something which is the essence of motivation; responding to man and circumstance. Try this: "Hi I am _____, and I am addicted to _____." Is there a self-help group nearby? You are being *motivated*!

Oh, brother! Here we go again! Yes, it is time to step back and address the personal inventory once again.

What are you *compelled* to do? What is it that you just cannot do without? What activity in which you participate causes hatred, discord, dissension, factions, or fits of rage? What are you using as an escape mechanism? What is it that you chase after? What *motivational* item or circumstances do feel as though you just could not give up to facilitate becoming an *inspiration* to those around you??

"Cast your cares on the LORD, and he will sustain you; he will never let the righteous be shaken."
                    (Psalm 55:22)

The term "cast" is a shepherding term that designates that a sheep has rolled over on its back and cannot, under its own power, right itself. It must be rescued by the shepherd, or there will be a certainty of death. The shepherd will pick up the sheep, massage its legs, and stand it in an upright position, returning him to the flock. That is why the shepherd will leave the ninety-nine to find the one lost sheep. That sheep might be cast down! A sheep that is cast is subject to any prey that lurks.

Our Good Shepherd, Jehovah Rohi, will take the cares that you cast upon Him and let them die (Saved). He will return you to an upright position (Righteous) promises Jehovah-Tsidkenu… I am the Lord thy God who will make you righteous.

"I am the good shepherd. The good shepherd lays down his life for the sheep.
                    (John 10:11)

"I am the good shepherd; I know my sheep and my sheep know me"
                    (John 10:16)

"My sheep listen to my voice; I know them, and they follow me."
                    (John 10:27)

64

10 TRUTH VS JEALOUSY & ENVY

INSPIRATION .... TRUTH

An inspired individual will always seek the truth, love the truth, and protect the truth.

The word "truth" always reminds me of the classic '50's television show Dragnet. Officer Joe Friday would interview witnesses and his infamous line was, "Just the facts ma'am, just the facts." Sergeant Friday wasn't interested in the opinions or supposition of the witness. He only wanted the truth; the actual details of the event that are factual and pertinent to the case.

The essential part of that interview process is that without the "facts," *conviction* would not be possible. Facts are the "truth of the matter." In a court of law, we swear to tell the truth, the whole truth, and nothing but the truth. The judge ensures that the attorneys do not lead a witness in their cross-examination or motivate them to give false testimony. That would be *"leading"* the witness. A conviction does not depend on conclusions, supposition, imagination, or second-hand information. It must be given by the witness and sworn to be true. Without the oath, a witness could perjure themselves without any fear of ramifications.

The jury is the only facet of the court process that renders the opinion based on the facts presented to them by the attorneys and their witnesses. The jury renders the *verdict*. They render that verdict based on a unanimous interpretation of the facts as has been presented. They, alone, have the power to *convict*. They cannot convict if there is a "reasonable doubt" that the defendant might be innocent.

If one leads a life of *Inspiration*, reasonable doubt does not exist. Quite simply, if the Spirit gives unction to make a choice or exercise discernment concerning the implications of motivational circumstances, there is no doubt that the prompting of the Spirit only serves the will of the Father. The Spirit has no room for reasonable doubt or negotiation.

Please let me re-emphasize the fact that the Spirit will never .... NEVER direct you toward a choice or decision that doesn't glorify the Father. There is absolutely no reason to ever doubt the leading of the Holy Spirit. Does the Spirit's leading consistently line up with OUR will? Absolutely not! When our will and the will of the Father are congruent, the Spirit's leading is an unstoppable force.

It has been said millions of times that, "the truth shall set you free." That IS the truth! When the truth comes forth, there is no need to carry the burden of being suspect in your statements or actions. There is a physical response that we each make when we tell the truth. Conversely, when we lie, it has a specific response as well. A lie detector can record it immediately. The truth will set you free without question.

I've always thought that a "lie detector test" would be better referred to as a "truth detector test." Detecting the truth is far more productive than detecting a lie. It is much like the training that a bank teller receives in order to recognize a counterfeit bill. The teller counts, by hand, an enormous quantity of real bills, one by one. The teller becomes so used to the feel of the real bills that when a counterfeit bill comes through, it just doesn't "feel" right, making it counterfeit. Recognizing untruth becomes rather easy when we are sensitive to the Spirit.

Motivators are sometimes experts at using untruth to entice you to buy into their agenda. An inspired individual will know in their gut that there is something that just doesn't feel right. The Spirit will alert you. Life provided many opportunities to discern the "real stuff." The Spirit will lead us to the right choice if we listen and feel his direction.

I would have to say that one of the most interesting training programs that I have been privileged to participate in was the study of body language. Body language is absolutely fascinating and extremely revealing, and I continue to benefit from almost daily.

As a corporate trainer, my study of body language and its purposes were varied. Let me share with you a brief example. Let's stop by HotShot Motor Company for a few minutes and exercise body language study as truth gathering.

Today I am a "mystery shopper." Mr. Ross has hired me to engage as a customer with one of his salespersons who seems to always cause great confusion with his customers. This salesperson seems to create a great deal of dissatisfaction. Mr. Ross is concerned that this particular salesperson will eventually cost the dealership its credibility. Mr. Ross could fire him, but he wants to make sure that he gives him the benefit of the doubt. He wants the facts; just the facts. Let's go in...

I enter the showroom and ask for the salesperson specifically. He is paged to come to the front desk. Mr. Rogers comes quickly to meet his new prospect at the desk. He introduces himself, and I return the gesture as we shake hands. He then asks, "What brings you here to see me today?" I respond with a statement that is designed to test his physical responses, "I believe it was your ad." Ducking his head, he replies, "Glad to know it is paying off."

He turns his back to me as we stroll to his desk, and speaks to me over his shoulder, "Is this your first visit to our dealership?" "Oh no," I reply. Still, with his back to me, he says, "It seems as though I have met you before." I respond, "I don't believe that we have ever met."

As we reach his desk, he plops down in his chair. Looking up at me he asks, "Well, what can I do for you today?" Not yet invited to do so, I go ahead and sit down in front of his desk as he leans back rocking in his desk chair, with his sloppy attitude, and with his hands folded behind his head.

I reply, "I'm looking for a car that I could buy for my daughter to drive back and forth to college." He leans forward with both elbows on the desk and says, "We have the best deals in the area." He gave me an answer that I didn't solicit. He did not honor my answer or my intent at all. He began to sell me on the dealership and his level of honesty and outstanding performance with his customers. I would be no exception... of course.

As he continued his self-promotion address, I noticed several typewritten letters pinned to his cubicle walls. Each letter was a thank you note for his very valuable service. Each letter had been mailed to him from his valued customers. He pointed them out to me with great pride, and with a sweeping hand states, "Satisfied customers!"

STOP! I could go on and on about this encounter but let's look at a few items that "spoke" to me in only a very few minutes:

My first impression of Mr. Rogers was less than impressive from the onset of our encounter. When he came to meet me, he had an arrogant swagger that spoke loudly of his perceived self-importance. He leaned backward when we shook hands which indicated that he was not going to be engaging on his part. Instead of walking beside me as we went to his desk, I trailed along behind him which was a control technique that would possibly set the stage for me to do the same (if I would allow him) all the way through the sales process. His body language spoke volumes. Foul body language!

When asked how I came to ask for him I stated that I had seen his ad, he responded by nodding his head in an up and down "Yes" manner, and stated, "I'm glad that is paying off." He, in fact, had no ad running in any publication, nor in the broadcast media. Dropping his head and averting eye contact with me indicated that was lying from the beginning. Speaking to me over his shoulder was not only rude but terribly evasive.

When reaching his desk, he did not invite me to sit but plopped down in his chair, tilted back, with his arms folded like wings and continued his diatribe; not a good impression for any potential client and very unprofessional.

The hammer fell hard when he pointed out the customer letters on the walls of his cubicle. These were the letters that he stated had been mailed to him extolling his stellar service. Why was that the clincher? Why was I suspect?

Well, if those letters had actually been mailed to him, they would have been folded. There was not a crease on them at all. Now, granted they could have all been sent in a 9x12 flat envelope, but I somehow seriously doubt it. The typeface font and paper stock would have varied.

FACT: He had typed those letters himself, and they had never mailed from anywhere; what a real deceiver and a terrible con-man. Mr. Rogers dealt his death blow in just a manner of minutes from the moment we met. His lack of professionalism, lack of listening skills, and inability, to tell the truth, would certainly have cost him a sale with the most tolerant customer.

Oh sure, I know that all car salespeople are considered liars, but let me assure you that perception is absolutely not true. There are some very fine folks, like Brad, who display professionalism and courtesy.

One bad apple CAN spoil the whole bunch though. Mr. Rogers was that bad apple at the HotShot Motor Company… or… WAS… at the HotShot Motor Company.

As an *inspired* individual, you can be assured that the Spirit within you will make sure you have that "gut feeling" when the truth is not being told and someone is trying to *motivate* you. How you choose to handle *man and circumstance* in these situations will set you apart by not responding in the same manner. Remember! It is not your job to convict the offender. That job belongs to the judge and jury: only test the spirit.

"Guide me in your truth and teach me, for you are God my Savior, and my hope is in you all day long."
(Psalm 25:5)

"Truthful lips endure forever, but a lying tongue lasts only a moment."
(Proverbs 12:19)

"Give glory to God by telling the truth."
(John 9:24)

"But when he, the Spirit of truth, comes, he will guide you into all the truth. He will not speak on his own"
(John 16:13)

There are many individuals and institutions that actually promote the use of half-truths, speculation and, innuendo. In this day and time, truth doesn't seem to matter, but it always matters greatly. There is an attitude that follows another old adage; "If you tell a lie long enough, people will start to believe it." Actually, YOU will begin to believe it.

The truth will set you free from worry and doubt. Many worrisome thoughts can be squelched by remembering this test of your thoughts;

"Is it Fact, Fiction, or Fantasy?"

As an *inspired* individual, we must test everything we think, do, or say. Perhaps it might be time to rid your thoughts of "stinking thinking." Be completely sure that what you think, say, and act upon is a result of absolute truth and will, without any doubt glorify God.

Here are some excellent examples of thought processes that you will want to avoid.... They very well may be *fiction or fantasy...* Just the facts!

Assumptions
Suppositions
Conjecture
Opinions
Speculations
Innuendo
Suspicions
Insinuations
Allusions
Notions

70

I can promise you that you will not win a contest if any results of the above just happen to be correct. No gold star is awaiting you. The initiation of the mental process, rooted in any of the above, will not glorify God in any way.

"And the peace of God, which transcends all understanding,
will guard your hearts and your minds in Christ Jesus."
(Philippians 4:6)

MOTIVATION.... ENVY & JEALOUSY

One of the oddest things that I have noticed during all my years of ministry is the observation that so many people, no matter how blessed, talented, or gifted they are, still lust after the talents and gifting of others. Often this mindset causes that individual to attempt to operate outside of their "job description" causing great confusion. I suppose that, even for His sheep, the grass always looks greener on the other side of the fence. Singers want to preach. Preachers want to sing. Teachers want to administrate. Administrators want to teach. Everyone wants to do someone else's job instead of focusing on the responsibilities they have been given.

Do you remember what my Dad told me? "The greatest source of frustration in anyone's life is when someone operates outside of their job description." You can rest assured that if you or someone else operates outside of their job description problems will follow. It may not be immediately evident, but resentment may be buried just below the surface struggling to get out! Mind your own business and mind it well. If we do our job at the optimum pitch, I doubt if we will have any time to interfere with the tasks of others.

It is wise to "help" only when help is asked for. It is also wise to do your job to the best of your ability before you begin to "train" others.

I've rarely witnessed anyone who didn't have to climb the corporate ladder one step at a time (unless you are owner's son, of course).

Lust is the driving force behind these scenarios. If one lusts for power, fame, fortune, notoriety, possessions, and accolades, it will leave the door wide open for every imaginable form of *motivation*. When is enough … enough? A lust-filled person is never satisfied.

Lust's evil twin is *envy*. Envy lurks in the heart and views what others *have* and desires to have it, even if they have to take it from them. How that acquisition occurs has no boundaries; whatever it takes!

The motivators in your life are fairly evident when they operate. Those who have lust and envy for your gifts, talents, or blessings will tip their hand at some point.

Envy and lust are not just evident in the corporate world, but often evident in the family and the church. "In my church? Are you kidding? No way! That is not possible!" Oh really? I believe that you might find that very scenario displayed at an event that occurred during a meal with Jesus and his disciples.

"An argument started among the disciples as to which of them would be the greatest. Jesus, knowing their thoughts, took a little child and had him stand beside him.

Then he said to them, "Whoever welcomes this little child in my name welcomes me, and whoever welcomes me welcomes the one who sent me. For it is the one who is least among you, who is the greatest."
(Luke 9:46)

Yes, even among the disciples there was a desire for someone to be number one.

"…make it your ambition to lead a quiet life:
You should mind your own business and work with your hands…"
(1 Thessalonians 4:11)

11 SELF CONTROL

S ELF CONTROL
is the most effective weapon that we have in our arsenal to vanquish *motivation* with *inspiration*. Self-control is the final step in displaying an inspirational lifestyle; the foundation of Inspiration.

Self-control is an all-encompassing tool of inspiration. It calls upon us to maintain absolute submission to the Spirit's leading. We must let the Spirit control every facet of our choices, encounters, and responses.

Self-control isn't just about grinning and bearing it, or gritting your teeth and repeating, "I'm not gonna do it!" over and over in your mind. Self-control doesn't cause you to be overwrought. In fact, self-control enables you to be totally at peace when you face the challenges of motivational circumstances and *motivators*.

Self-control is, quite simply, being predisposed to knowing how you will handle *motivation* when it rears its ugly head. The fruit of the flesh is evident in every motivational offering, and the temptation is the heartbeat of every motivating circumstance. Knowing ahead of time, as to how you will respond to motivation, enables you to listen to that "small voice" of the Spirit and then respond appropriately. Be prepared.

Self-control is not self-denial. In fact, the only thing you will deny yourself is the "opportunity" to deal with the problems that motivation creates without a provocative response. Self-control is the perfect opportunity to demonstrate meekness; *Power under control.*

When motivation/temptation arises, you must have a prepared response. If you are offered anything that would be harmful to you physically, mentally, or spiritually be prepared to reject the offer with a spirit-led rebuff.

"Anyone who is never at fault in what they say is perfect, able to keep their whole body in check. When we put bits into the mouths of horses to make them obey us, we can turn the whole animal. Or take ships as an example. Although they are so large and are driven by strong winds, they are steered by a very small rudder wherever the pilot wants to go. Likewise, the tongue is a small part of the body, but it makes great boasts. Consider what a great forest is set on fire by a small spark. The tongue also is a fire, a world of evil among the parts of the body. It corrupts the whole body, sets the whole course of one's life on fire, and is itself set on fire by hell."
(James 3:2-6)|

12 INTERMISSION

Now, let's take a brief intermission and review some key points of the contrasting dynamics of Inspiration vs Motivation.

Your choices will determine the quality of your life's experience.

Choose wisely!

It is time to revisit that personal self-inventory to ensure that the right Spirit is within you in which will facilitate the dynamics of *Inspiration*.

How have you responded, thus far, to the preceding text?

Are you experiencing revelation or agitation? Are you the motivator?

Which motivators have you identified that seem to keep your life off balance?

Who or what are the primary motivators that hold you hostage on a regular basis? Are you prepared to deal with them now?

Are you absolutely positive that the right Spirit lives within you?

Will you allow the Holy Spirit to be evident in every aspect of your life?

Inspiration	Motivation
Root word: Spirit	Root word: Motive
A response to the Spirit within Produces:	A response to man or circumstance Produces:
Peace	Fear
Love	Hatred
Joy	Discord
Gentleness	Dissension
Meekness	Factions
Kindness	Selfish-Ambition
Goodness	Fits Of Rage
Patience	Addictions
Truth	Jealousy and Envy
Self-Control	Idolatry
Becomes Proactive	Becomes Reactive
"Against these things, there is no law"	"For those who live like will not inherit the kingdom of God."
Galatians 5:22	Galatians 5:19
Abundant Life	Abundant Strife

Without the leading of the Holy Spirit (Inspiration), it is impossible to respond properly to the motivational circumstances you will encounter. You will lead a life of manipulation responding to outside influences.

13 PRODUCE – THE HARVEST

My hometown of Hendersonville, NC has been renowned for years as one of the largest apple producers in the country. Henderson County ranks seventh in all the apple producing counties in America. Henderson County produces 65% of all of the apples grown in North Carolina. The apple industry is a twenty-two million dollar industry in Henderson County.

Apples brought John Peter Corn, commissariat to George Washington, to the mountains of western Carolina after the Revolutionary War. He and his brother Jesse foraged for supplies for George Washington's army at Valley Forge. They discovered a vast supply of apples in the hills of Carolina. At the end of the war, George Washington offered land grants to both brothers in the place of their choosing. They chose the mountains of Carolina. The old home place of the Corn family is right there in Hendersonville, NC, my hometown. John Peter Corn is buried in the Ebenezer Baptist Church Cemetery with a gravestone identifying him as a Revolutionary War soldier. John Peter planted some good seed in his time. The Corn family has given more preachers to western North Carolina than any other single family.

As a young boy, I became self-sufficient pretty early in life. I loved to work. One of my jobs each summer was to work in the apple packing houses. My job was to separate the sizes of the apples and cull the apples that weren't visually attractive for retail sale. These ugly apples would be used as "juicers." They may not have been the type of apple you would see displayed at the grocer's produce department, but those apples had great value by being turned into apple juice. The juicing companies that are located in Hendersonville produce an average of two million gallons of juice per year derived from 525,000 bushels of apples. Good fruit, ugly or not, always has value. Bad fruit.... well, NEVER!

The following chapters will illuminate the "produce" of your *Inspired* choices and responses, as well as the produce of your *Motivated* choices and responses and their ultimate ramifications. The following is the produce from the seeds that you will plant. This produce will allow you to *test the Spirit* of every choice or response you might encounter.

The laws of "seed, time, and harvest" are operating not only in agriculture but human nature as well. Every apple contains seeds that will, when planted, produce an entire tree that will produce a harvest of more apples containing seeds, which replicates the process over and over again. Hey! That's better than any multi-level marketing plan!

Good seed sown will produce good fruit. Conversely, bad seed sown will produce bad fruit. That is the law of seed, time, and harvest.

"As long as the earth endures, seed, time and harvest, cold and heat,
summer and winter, day and night, will never cease."
(Genesis 8:22

The Produce of

Inspiration and *Motivation*

14 FREEDOM VS BONDAGE

INSPIRATION…. FREEDOM

An inspired choice always creates freedom. As Galatians 5:21 states; "Against these things, there is no law." If there is no law against something, then there is no condemnation, no trial, no conviction, and no incarceration. We are not in bondage in any way. We are free!

When we make inspired choices, we never have to defend ourselves. We are free to move forward in our lives with no looking back. We can look through the windshield instead of the rearview mirror.

Granted, we may have someone or something nipping at our heels, but it is not our problem. It is a problem of someone else in response to our inspired choice. It should be glaringly evident in today's society that you can be despised for making choices to do what is right.

In today's society, a person's "rights" are more important to them than doing what IS right.

It is quite gratifying when you choose to respond to the Spirit's guidance within you. You will find that you will stand upright and you will have some pep in your step. You'll walk with pride.

MOTIVATION.... BONDAGE

The instant an individual promotes or responds to motivation *bondage* arrives on the scene. Again, motivation is a response to man and circumstance. If someone *motivates* you, the flesh will rise up immediately. Responding with *inspiration* overcomes that.

When we survey the list of the fruits of the flesh, it is very easy to see what the results could be. Bondage arrives in many packages. Motivated actions are often the precipitate of former motivations.

John wants to keep up with the Jones'. John purchases a home in the Jones' very expensive neighborhood. He is very envious of their affluent lifestyle and seeks that same lifestyle for himself. To pay for that new home, new car, new boat, and wave runner he must make more money to keep up these appearances. He then fuels his self-ambition with a feverish work ethic which causes great discord in his home. His wife receives the brunt of his fits of rage when he comes home so late at night tired and disgruntled.

He has started drinking heavily to cope with the self-imposed pressure and has found some relief in the company of a younger woman that works in the office. He has become more and more fearful and hateful to those around him. Guilt abounds!

And whose fault is it? HIS WIFE, of course!! Why yes! He is doing it ALL for her. Yeah right!! In his mind, "It's ALL her fault!" Not so! It is his fault completely. Motivation gives birth to more motivation.

Bondage comes in many forms, but there is one common thread that runs throughout each one of them... SELF!

Self-centered people are without accountability. A self-centered person puts themselves in bondage, but it is always the fault of someone else. They are never accountable or responsible.

15 PRO-ACTIVE VS RE-ACTIVE

INSPIRATION....PRO-ACTIVE

The inspired individual is *Pro-Active* and never becomes easy prey to a motivator. A pro-active individual is a self-starter who follows the leading of the Spirit from within and accomplishes the task at hand with great dedication and zeal. Pro-Active individuals don't have to be told what to do to be successful. They actively seek a path to accomplishing their goals and dreams. Their success is gauged on various levels, and they do not necessarily define their success as financial. They define success on a larger scope by seeking redemptive goals and results.

They are very teachable, readily respond to their training, and move forward on their own initiative with the leading of the Spirit. They aren't "hyper"... they are busy looking forward, pressing toward the mark.

Pro-active people don't need an incentive to excel. They take great pride in their accomplishments and protect that which they have built which honors God and produces an awareness of the Fruit Of The Spirit.

Reactive people are not positive self-starters. They must be presented with something that benefits them to force them into action. There has to be something to give them the incentive to do what it supposed to be done.

Reactive people are naturally very "reactionary." They will exhibit every trait in the list of the fruit of the flesh in their thoughts and actions. They are costly the family, the workplace, and probably the church.

Reactive people are prone to fly off the handle, in a fit of rage, at the least little thing that doesn't go their way. They experience hatred for themselves and others. They are fearful of failure and the ramifications that follow if they should fail. That fear causes them to become selfishly ambitious overachievers who will climb over anyone, at any cost, to get what they want, or they won't try at all. They create dissension among their family and their workplace. They are prone to addictions to cope with their fears and guilt. They are swelled with bravado, but in reality, they suffer from low self-esteem. They are envious and jealous and may be prone to invest in material things to attempt to portray a grander lifestyle than they can afford. They are often thieves.

In today's culture, we are developing a society of grossly re-active individuals. Young and old alike have become addicted to electronic devices control their lives. Hours and hours each day are spent interacting with video games, phones, social media, and many other digital interests. Their brains are being re-wired in their thought processes and are then finding that they just can't exist without their phone, pad, or game controllers. They are certainly addicted; severely!

Youth spend an enormous amount of time each day playing video games that are totally "reactive." The result is a culture of children who seemingly have no inspiration and have to be motivated to do most anything at all.

Creativity is lost, and human interaction suffers greatly.

The instant the "Start" button is pressed, every move from that point is *reactive*. The player is reacting to what the computer does inside the game's software. There is no true value in these games at all. To garner the highest score is no testimony of greatness. There is no intrinsic value whatsoever, but an alternate reality is created. Pro-activity is lost! Creativity is lost! Personal interaction is lost!

Are you finding that your employees are less and less productive? Check their social media involvement. Ban phone usage in the workplace until their break or lunchtime.

Want to have dinner with the family at a local restaurant without the glow of cell phones in their faces? Try this! Stack everyone's phone in the middle of the table. The first one to use or answer their phone pays the tab!

Are you finding that your children have to be incentivized to have them perform their responsibilities? Use the digital media situation as a reward system and ban digital media usage after a specified time.

Remove these devices from them entirely and see just how reactive they will become! You might want to stand back first! KABOOM!

In 2006, a Newsweek magazine dedicated an entire edition to the study of the diminishing scores and graduate levels from high school the boys from age ten to eighteen were experiencing. They deemed the two greatest causes to be video games and absentee fathers.

Being Pro-Active or Re-active boils down to one common denominator: Choices! As a parent choose wisely. As an adult become proactive!

16 CONVICTED VS CONVINCED

INSPIRATION....CONVICTED

If we were sitting in a courtroom, the last word in the world we would want to hear from the judge would be, "CONVICTED!"

That type of *conviction* could have some serious consequences. The chances are that we could even lose our freedom. To reach this type of conviction would be a very involved process; arrested, charged, presentation of evidence that would prove an individual guilty, people to bear witness to the facts of the case, arguments by opposing attorneys, deliberation by a jury of one's peers rendering a verdict.... GUILTY! Convicted!

Thankfully, it is a good thing that the conviction of the Holy Spirit does not operate that way. Operating under *inspiration* ensures that we will NOT be condemned by the most powerful judge in the universe; the Lord God Almighty! The conviction of the Holy Spirit always points us in the right direction enabling us to glorify God.

"....there is now no condemnation for those who are in Christ Jesus"
(Romans 8:1)

Remember! *"Against these things (Fruit Of The Spirit) there is no law."*
(Galatians 5:23)

We can rest assured that when we operate our lives under the banner of inspiration that the only conviction we will experience is the conviction of the Holy Spirit. The Spirit will guide us in the right path. Our choices and responses to outside stimulus will be guided by the Holy Spirit and produce attitudes that will glorify God. The Spirit will only convict you to make *right* choices. Sin cannot be in the presence of God, so the Spirit will only guide you to redemptive acts, as God orders your steps.

*"When you walk, your **steps** will not be hampered; when you run, you will not stumble."*
(Proverbs 4:12)

Inspiration is a response to the Spirit. Trust it! Test the spirit of every choice and chose to be inspired. You cannot lose. He promises that!

MOTIVATION.... CONVINCED

A true conviction will never come from a motivator. You will easily discern that a motivating individual will make every effort to "convince" you to make a choice that will benefit the motivator or his or her desires. Don't buy into the motivator and his or her personal agenda.

It has been a while since we stopped by the HotShot Motor Company. Let's see what the folks are up to today. Oh! I see Jay!! Jay is on the lot greeting a new customer. Let's listen in....

90

"Good afternoon folks, I am Jay, how may I help you today?" The customer replies, "Oh, we are just looking." Jay meets that statement with the standard line, "That's great! Sure glad you stopped by, we have the best prices in town. Are you looking for a car or truck?" "Well, we aren't sure. We will know it when we see it," the customer states, hoping Jay will disappear and allow them to look around and discuss their needs. Jay says enthusiastically, "Let me show you the best deal on the lot," as he turns to walk toward a sleek silver sedan.

Jay fully expects that they will follow him to the sedan like lost puppies. He knows that this particular car has been sitting on the lot for three months and there is a sizable bonus on the car for the salesman that sells it. Yes, sir! It is the best deal on the lot….You bet! ….for JAY!!

Jay begins his pitch as to the equipment, mileage, previous owner and the incredible deal that it would be for them (and for Jay). "If I could make this car affordable for you would you buy this car today?" The customers are silent. Jay wonders, "What is wrong? I gave them the information about the car and the fact it would be a good deal for them….Hummmm?? What is missing? What is going wrong?"

What is wrong is the fact that Jay is much more interested in trying to convince them to purchase *that* particular car rather than asking qualifying questions that would reveal their actual needs, in which, would then dictate what type of vehicle was required for their family. Unknown to Jay is the fact they have five children of a wide age range, so size matters. Jay failed to ask any questions that would indicate what their needs were. The customers leave bewildered.

Jay is perplexed as to why they left and didn't buy that four-door. He just couldn't *convince* them to buy. He didn't put their needs first!

It is pretty hard to live through single a day without someone trying to convince you of something; buy the "new and improved", your raise will be delayed due to the economy, if you send the television evangelist your money then your anointed prayer cloth ill arrive that will solve all of your problems, your daughter wants to move in with her boyfriend because it will be much more economical if they share the rent, your driveway needs a $2000 sealant applied, your vacation worries are over if you will just buy that time-share deal, that toothpaste will make your smile brighter, video games increase hand to eye co-ordination, and your neighbor will bring your lawn mower back tomorrow. Right!

There is a Hebrew word for that pronounced; Boccckk-Low-Nay... Here in the South, we call it BAH-LONE-A! Baloney! Pure ole baloney!

The Spirit will give you clear conviction in your choices. You will not need an outside interpreter to convince you as to what you should do.

Just wait for the Spirit's conviction. It will be well worth the wait!

17 TEMPERED VS TEMPTED

INSPIRATION.... TEMPERED

An inspired individual will stand the test of time, walking through the fires of trials and struggles, while trusting God to bring him or her through it. It sounds implausible to embrace those difficult times with joy, but the Bible admonishes us to exactly that;

"Consider it pure joy, my brothers, and sisters, whenever you face trials of many kinds because you know that the testing of your faith produces perseverance. Let perseverance finish its work so that you may be mature and complete, not lacking anything. If any of you lacks wisdom, you should ask God, who gives generously to all without finding fault, and it will be given to you. But when you ask, you must believe and not doubt, because the one who doubts is like a wave of the sea, blown and tossed by the wind. That person should not expect to receive anything from the Lord. Such a person is double-minded and unstable in all they do."

(James 1:2-8)

"Blessed is the one who perseveres under trial because, having stood the test, that person will receive the crown of life that the Lord has promised to those who love him."

(James 1:12)

An *inspired* individual becomes tempered just like steel. Steel is heated to a very high degree point which causes the steel to be more flexible and less rigid and brittle. As an inspired individual, we should fully realize that we will encounter some serious heat from Motivators. Consider those times as *tempering* moments that will allow you to less rigid and brittle, and more discerning. You will be able to be more flexible as you follow the Spirit's leading. Those times will give you the understanding, that to maintain a high degree of flexibility, the "heat" is necessary as well for your strength. Being tempered allows us the flexibility to embrace the possibility that there could be *redemption* rather than *rejection*.

MOTIVATION.... TEMPTED

If there were an alternate title of this book, it just might be "How To Deal With The Temptation Of The Motivations In The World." That is a bit long for the title, but the message is clear; how do I deal with the temptation that motivating circumstances impose on me?

Motivators and motivating circumstances will tempt us to make some very bad choices if we try retaliation. For inspiration to triumph over motivation, we cannot fall prey to the motivator or the circumstances. The moment we try to retaliate, we are toast! We are motivators too.

It is imperative that we learn to not respond to the temptation in any way that would compromise our inspired lifestyle.

Just as many lives have been ruined by the *motivated* individual when they are tempted to retaliate after having become the victim of *motivating circumstances*.

94

It would take a thousand pages to list all of the temptations that could be nipping at our heels. You are equipped by the Holy Spirit to contend with each of them even though you would love to respond in like kind. It is useless to honor motivation with a response other than what the Spirit provides.

"Weak people get revenge. Strong people forgive. Intelligent people ignore." – Albert Einstein

Sure, I understand that you think you just might choke to death on the words that are gripping your throat. But, I promise you that nothing good will ever come from a motivated response. Remember that it is virtually impossible to reason with the unreasonable.

"No temptation has overtaken you except what is common to mankind. And God is faithful; he will not let you be tempted beyond what you can bear. But when you are tempted, he will also provide a way out so that you can endure it."
(1 Corinthians 10:13)

Self-control is the spiritual dynamic that will enable you to withstand any temptation that is imposed upon you. If you are predisposed to knowing how to respond to temptation, you will be able to exhibit self-control when you have a prepared answer to offer with the Spirit's leading.

"But when you are tempted, he will also provide a way out so that you can endure it."
(1 Corinthians 10:13)

18 CONSTRUCTIVE VS DESTRUCTIVE

INSPIRATION…. CONSTRUCTIVE

Inspired individuals will enjoy their *produce* as their choices are constructive. They build up rather than tear down. Their outlook is such that it is well beyond the "optimistic." Optimism is simply a matter of intense hope. There is still a modicum of risk involved in being simply optimistic in one's choices where inspired choices extend beyond hope and embrace the extension of faith; TRUST. An inspired individual trusts the Spirit to guide to a place where God's plans are to be revealed.

There are some folks who meet any thought of an idea moving forward with immediate resistance. For some people, resistance is a matter of habit. They feel that illuminating all of the things that could go wrong should be discussed before they are even aware of the benefits of the idea proposed. Inundated with "What ifs…" and fear, they stall the process of forwarding positive movement. If the Spirit gives unction, rest assured, resistance will follow to slow the process to a crawl. It may even prevent our taking the very steps that God has prepared for us.

On Chuck Swindoll's book, "Three Steps Forward – Two Steps Back" the back cover grabbed my attention when he made this statement:

"Many of life's greatest opportunities are cleverly disguised as impossible situations."

The title alone describes exactly how inspired individuals have to deal with following the leading of the Spirit. There seems to be a motivator lurking in the shadows to attempt to diminish the forward progress every time. Testing the Spirit of the resistance can be attributed to various fruits of the flesh; not the least of which is *fear*.

Overcoming motivation in the circumstances like these requires the inspired individual to call on the power of the Spirit to push through the negative atmosphere to accomplish God's plan. We cannot cower down and knuckle under the resistance that the *motivator* will use against us. We must press on with the assurance and satisfaction that we are moving forward for the glory of God's kingdom.

Perhaps the resistance comes from a trusted advisor? Never abandon God's plan for anyone or anything. Your trusted advisor may be responding from his or her past experience causing the fear that you may fail as he or she did. That is not uncommon at all. We may be fearless in our pursuit of the Spirit's leading, but those we love may be fearful that we might fail and be hurt or disappointed. If the Spirit is leading us, how can we truly fail? If we believe that God orders our steps how can we doubt? Are we to dodge His leading if He tells us to "take joy in trials and tribulations?" We will surely encounter resistance, but we do not have to be defeated!

*"What, then, shall we say in response to these things? If God is for us, who can be against us? He who did not spare his own Son, but gave him up for **us** all—how will he not also, along with him, graciously give **us** all things? Who will bring any charge against those whom God has chosen?"*

(Romans 8:31-39)

"The LORD *makes firm the steps of the one who delights in Him."*
(Psalm 37:23)

MOTIVATION…. DESTRUCTIVE

As I view our country today, I see so many motivating circumstances that are causing vast destruction to our American way of life. The very foundations this country embraced at its very inception has brought our country to a standard of excellence that is envied around the world. America is the greatest place in the world to live.

My personal family heritage provides me with great pride and respect for what has been built over these two centuries. I am reminded of an old adage I heard years ago that rings true today;

"What one generation will build, the next generation will protect, and the next generation will squander."

Today's circumstances are highly motivated and embracing the fruit of the flesh. From our homes to our communities, to our national stage, we are living in the squandering generation.

For the demolition of any building, a demolition company will set off the explosives at the foundation. When ignited the foundation crumbles and the net result is the building comes down on itself. Implosion!

The foundations of our faith, the foundations of our families, and the foundations of our most cherished institutions are being attacked as we stand idly by allowing it to happen. Aren't we called to be good stewards of what God has provided for us? I certainly think so!

There are so many destructive motivational circumstances that are attacking our lives each day. They can become overwhelming. What are we to do to overcome these situations? ... BE INSPIRED!!

*"Do not be overcome by **evil**, but overcome evil with good."*
(Romans 12:21)

"I have told you these things, so that in me you may have peace. In this world, you will have trouble. But take heart! I have overcome the world."
(John 16:33)

"Who is it that overcomes the world? Only the one who believes that Jesus is the Son of God."
(1 John 5:5)

Build up! Do not tear down! Hold on to your cherished, heartfelt values. Do not let go of them! Stand firm and resolute, not allowing the motivations of the world overcome you. Stand tall! Stand firm!

19 GOD'S GUIDANCE VS MAN'S ENABLEMENT

INSPIRATION…. SEEKING GOD'S GUIDANCE

As an inspired individual, it seems out of reason that one could be reliant on anything but God's guidance. Regardless of years of experience or levels of education, proper choices and responses have to be derived from the leading of the Spirit.

I would hope that, as one becomes more and more sensitive to hearing that still small voice of the Spirit, God's guidance would become more apparent. Our hearts must be quickened to His voice.

There may have been times in your life where you knew that God led to something, but it didn't work out as you had planned. I love this quote that I found in a feel-good movie "Coffee Shop." The movie's setting is at a northeastern seaside inlet in Massachusetts. It was a quaint little hamlet that had the normal set of characters. The quote comes from a loving patron who is in a wheelchair. Max had hurt his back in a fall years before and came in every day for a mug of coffee in HIS   mug.

Donavan, a very sweet and beautiful young lady, is the owner of a lovely little coffee shop that she opened when she was only nineteen. The clientele that visited daily were her regulars, and she was loved very much by them all. Her quirky staff was very loyal and supported her in every way. Her beloved banker, who had supported her for all the past years, sold his bank. When the new banker reviewed her file, he decided that she would have to become current on her loan or they would foreclose on her shop property. Of course there were subplots galore but the prevailing plot was that her good looking, hot shot, fancy sports car driving boyfriend was working behind her back with the new banker to sell her property to a company for a huge profit (and a huge commission for himself of course) in order to tear down the building for a parking lot.

After her efforts to resolve the issue, she was exhausted and very despondent. Max rolls up on the dock in his wheelchair beside her car. As she is getting out, she looks frazzled and hopeless when Max says,

"Just because things aren't going as you planned, doesn't mean that things are not going as they should be."

That statement is profound. Even when we operate under Inspiration, it doesn't mean that our plans are going to always coincide with God's timeline. In these times we are required to trust Him the most.

God's guidance and wisdom are promised simply for the asking:

"But the wisdom that comes from heaven is first of all pure; then peace-loving, considerate, submissive, full of mercy and good fruit, impartial and sincere. Peacemakers who sow in peace reap a harvest of righteousness."
(James 3:14)

"If any of you lacks wisdom, you should ask God, who gives generously to all without finding fault, and it will be given to you."
(James 1:5)

Godly wisdom will accomplish your task. He will provide it for you for every choice that you encounter. Seek it! As He "orders our steps", it is imperative that we do not run ahead of His timeline.

Inspired individuals should always seek God's wisdom to vanquish the motivational tools used against them. Just ask! He WILL supply!

MOTIVATION.... RELYING ON MAN'S KNOWLEDGE

Motivated individuals and motivators do not seek God's guidance. Well, after all, they are "intelligent." Right? Sure they are! They have all the answers. They may have been educated in the top ivy league schools, but their "knowledge" will never trump God's wisdom.

Wisdom comes from God. Knowledge comes from the absorption of ideas, speculation, opinions, assumptions, and the experiences of man. Isn't it interesting that in the "knowledge" arena there are so many varying, and often opposing, ideas, speculation, opinions, assumptions, and experiences that cause; hatred, discord, dissension, factions, fits of rage, selfish ambition, addictions, impurity, and the lingering doubt as to what is truth? God's wisdom never contradicts itself. His wisdom is not a matter of argument, but a matter of fact.

"For the foolishness of God is wiser than human wisdom, and the weakness of God is stronger than human strength."
(1 Corinthians 1:25)

"Observe them carefully, for this will show your wisdom and understanding to the nations, who will hear about all these decrees and say, 'Surely this great nation is a wise and understanding people.'"
(Deuteronomy 4:6)

*"God gave Solomon **wisdom** and very great insight, and a breadth of understanding as measureless as the sand on the seashore."*
(1 Kings 4:29)

Knowledge refined through wisdom is powerful and glorifying to His kingdom, but knowledge without having been refined through wisdom is a fool's paradise.

"Where is the wise person? Where is the teacher of the law? Where is the philosopher of this age? Has not God made foolish the wisdom of the world?"
(1 Corinthians 1:20)

Without question, this world is filled with people who deceive and attempt to motivate others with their supposed intellect. They seek to destroy the foundations of our faith and our country, in an effort to convince the people that, somehow in days passed, we got it all wrong.

I challenge that mindset with a very simple fact; be it our home, our business, or our country, the blessings that we have enjoyed would not have occurred without the guiding hand of God. Our enemies never seek to bless us, do they? As a country, we are the greatest benefactor on earth in their times of need. Remember! Motivated people are never thankful, but expect to be enabled and entitled. Immediately!

20 SELFLESSNESS VS SELFISHNESS

INSPIRATION…. SELFLESS

It is Monday morning at the HotShot Motor Company, and the sales meeting has just ended. Rick and Brad are heading toward the showroom. Rick is telling Brad about the great weekend that he and his wife had spent in the mountains. "It was really great to get away and spend some time by ourselves in the quiet of the mountains. Just to enjoy a couple of days without any interruptions was just what we needed."

Just as they entered the hallway, Rick notices that his numbers on the sales tote-board are two points higher than Thursday when he left.

Standing there he asks Brad, "How in the world did that happen?" Brad replied, "Oh I forgot to tell you this morning that you had a customer come in on Friday and another on Saturday that you have been working with for a couple of weeks, and they decided to buy. I knew you had been working those deals so I just closed them and put them in the finance office to do their paperwork while I got the cars ready for their delivery. I explained to them that you and your wife had an opportunity to get away to the mountains for the weekend, and they were happy for you. You'll want to call them and thank them for coming in, I'm sure."

Rick thankfully replied, "Oh man! I appreciate your handling them for me. The tote numbers should have gone up by only one number though." Brad happily said, "Oh no! I didn't split the deals with you. You got full credit for both deals. You've worked hard for those deals, and you really impressed your customers with your service to them. Having a weekend getaway didn't cost you a thing here. I wasn't busy at the times they came in and it didn't cost me anything but a little prep time. Maybe you'll do me a favor sometime."

SELFLESS! That Brad is just TOO nice!

Rick's weekend could have been costly for him had Brad not acted in such a selfless manner. The split commission could have cost him more than the cost of his weekend trip to the mountains. That would have sucked the joy right out of his heart and defeated the entire purpose of the trip. Brad's inspired response to the circumstances maintained the joy that Rick and his wife had shared in the mountains.

A selfless act simply puts others before your self. Granted, it is a rarity in these days and times, but there are some people who are willing to put others before themselves. Brad made an inspired choice that produced some good fruit. Well, after all, Brad is TOO NICE! It appears that he is also selfless, Brad chose to act in the way he did because he was responding to the Spirit within him.

You can bet that there were several others in the dealership that wouldn't have responded that way. In fact, they live on split deals. Someone does the homework, and they share the grade. Gladly!

MOTIVATION…. SELFISHNESS

Oh yes! There are those that benefit from the efforts of others. At the HotShot Motor Company, there is one individual, Ray, who has the reputation of having an orchestrated plan to always be in the showroom at the times the other salespeople step out to lunch or have a day off. He watches their deals and knows where they are in the process of closing the customer. He thrives on split deals with no apology.

He knows if a customer comes in and asks for their salesperson and they aren't there for some reason, he will go to no lengths to convince them to let him "help" the absent salesperson by helping them. Bingo! Split deal! His efforts are calculated. He has caused some of his fellow salespeople to have some expensive lunches by "skating" their customers.

These *motivators* are always ready to get, but rarely ready to give. They ring the bell when it comes to selfish ambition. These individuals have a false sense of security. They are painfully obvious and yet they believe that they are in "stealth mode." Ray always tries to benefit from others.

"I urge you, brothers and sisters, to watch out for those who cause divisions and put obstacles in your way that are contrary to the teaching you have learned. Keep away from them."
(Romans 16:17)

"Do nothing out of selfish ambition or vain conceit. Rather, in humility value others above yourselves."
(Philippians 2:3)

"For where you have envy and selfish ambition, there you find disorder and every evil practice."
(James 3:16)

21 UNITY VS UNIFORMITY

INSPIRATION…. UNITY

There are various words and phrases that describe unity; like-minded, in unison, in harmony, in one accord, in agreement to name a few. The most powerful unity is when we are "one in the Spirit." That form of unity transcends all other descriptions.

When inspired individuals work in harmony, the positive potential is beyond measure. Great things can be accomplished. A relationship, a work project, a business venture, even a sports activity has the greatest potential for success.

Regardless of physical, emotional, or denominational differences, great things can be accomplished if the Spirit is the driving force guiding the venture.

It is glaringly evident that the Fruit Of The Spirit is in operation and resistance has been virtually eliminated. What enormous freedom exists when the Spirit leads the relationship, the family, or the project. *"I urge you to live a life worthy of the calling you have received. Be completely humble and gentle; be patient, bearing with one another in love. Make every effort to keep the unity of the Spirit through the bond of peace."*

(Ephesians 4:2-3)

"How good and pleasant it is when God's people live together in unity!"
(Psalm 133:1)

We are one in the Spirit, we are one in the Lord
We are one in the Spirit, we are one in the Lord
And we pray that our unity will one day be restored
And they will know that we are Christians by our love, by our love
Yes, they will know that we are Christians by our love

We will work with each other, we will work side by side
We will work with each other, we will work side by side
And we'll guard each man's dignity and save each man's pride
And they will know that we are Christians by our love, by our love
Yeah, they will know that we are Christians by our love.

Songwriter: Peter Scholtes
They'll Know We Are Christians by Our Love lyrics © Music Services, Inc

The power of unity is enormous! An inspiring person can accomplish much if there is the common thread of the guidance of the Spirit. With a common goal, the results are astounding in any facet of life; relationships, family, business ventures, ministry opportunities, and any other collective group effort. Unity is ultimate synergy!

It is important to know that the individual's unity with the Spirit is the ultimate goal that produces inspiration and draws others to Him.

MOTIVATION....UNIFORMITY

Once again, it is very important to see the contrast between the words *unity* and *uniformity*. They are absolute opposites creating two different worldviews.

The world is motivated to be uniform; socially, politically, economically, and even spiritually. It is very easy to blend in with the masses and have very little in common with the majority of the others in the group. An individual can find themselves lost in a sea of idealism. There are those who would choose to be uniform to eliminate any pressure to excel and stand out in the crowd. They only want to blend in. Thus they are easily *motivated* to do so.

As an instructor, I witness this constantly. Many of my students do not want to excel to a point where they become "visible." Heaven forbid that a peer may find them exalted for their performance! "Well, what are you trying to be?" After all, isn't everyone supposed to get a trophy or a certificate of participation? Why do we give certificates for those that simply arrive and do what they are required to do?

Several years ago I had a young lady from a local high school who was a terrific music student. She was always prepared and accomplished her task every week and gave me great hope that she would someday utilize that talent to her advantage on a major scale. Her appearance was somewhat daunting in that she embraced the "uniform" of those of the Gothic lifestyle. Her "look" could be a hindrance in the future should she decide to pursue a legitimate musical career.

The school term was over, and in the very first session of the summer break, an absolutely beautiful girl came in the studio at her session time. This girl looked like a movie star! "Who is she?", I wondered.

When she spoke, I realized that it was the same girl that had been dressed as a Goth the entire year before! What an amazing transformation!

When I asked her about the change in appearance, she laughed and said, "Oh I just dressed that way so that everyone would leave me alone at school; including the teachers." She was using reverse-motivation. Based on the standards of her peers, she became *uniform* while maintaining a grade point average that placed her third in her graduating class. While attaining excellence, she found a way to escape the high school drama. I was totally intrigued as to how she developed her game plan to be drama-free. It was an oddly genius *performance* that dispelled any *drama*. BRAVO!

If the motivation of the world calls you just to blend in...DO NOT ANSWER THE CALL! Just let it ring! If you are an inspired individual, do not let the world drag you down when you have the potential for excellence. We are called to excellence in everything we do. Attain it! And remember

"The path to excellence is overgrown with the weeds of mediocrity!"
(Patrick L. Corn)

You do not have to blend in and become uniform in any way that diminishes your call to excellence or causes you to lose your identity.

"Finally, brothers and sisters, whatever is true, whatever is noble, whatever is right, whatever is pure, whatever is lovely, whatever is admirable—if anything is excellent or praiseworthy—think about such things."

(Philippians 4:8)

"This is a trustworthy saying. And I want you to stress these things, so that those who have trusted in God may be careful to devote themselves to doing what is good. These things are excellent and profitable for everyone."

(Titus 3:8)

22 SERVANTHOOD VS SERVITUDE

INSPIRATION.... SERVANTHOOD

For many people, the idea of servanthood follows a misconception that one must bow down and submit to the wishes of others. This mindset is derived from the idea that a "servant" is an individual who is indentured and must perform services for another individual because they are owed a debt, or are paid for their service, or are the victim of someone who controls their lives. This type of servant is "enslaved" or is hired to serve others. They are in bondage in one way or another. It is assumed that they are of a lower class and are subservient to their employer. They are someone's "step and fetch it." Whatever they do is demanded, and they have no choice but to perform their duties as required. This type of servant begrudges every function that they are required to do even if they were fully aware of the job description before they hired on to perform the task.

Truly inspired servanthood occurs when an individual has the unction from within to perform an act, for the benefit of another, without any type of provocation except the guidance of the Holy Spirit.

It is a selfless act that may well be inconvenient or completed unwarranted by anyone else. It is a loving choice for the benefit of another.

Brad is the kind of guy who has a servant's heart. Closing the two deals over the weekend for Rick, without any remuneration, was a perfect example of an inspired choice to benefit another. It is Brad's nature, and his actions will be a fine example for others in the dealership as they display true servanthood and good workplace community. He wasn't paid to serve Rick. He closed those deals for Rick because he knew how hard Rick had worked on them and it would be unfair for Rick to have to split the deal with someone else just because he was gone that weekend for a well-deserved outing. It was a magnanimous gesture on Brad's part to do that. That act shows what Brad is made of, and it's not just because he is "TOO nice." He is a true servant, and true servants are leaders.

There are those who are employed to serve the public. Well, after all, they are called a "Customer Service Representative"; a CSR. They like Bill, the Service Manager at HotShot Motors, rarely encounter customers that are glowingly satisfied. More often than not, they only deal with the complaints of the customers who are experiencing problems with a product or service. They stand to be *motivated* continuously. To be an effective CSR, it is required that you follow a prescribed protocol to resolve the issue. Even if they do resolve the problem, the customer is rarely fully satisfied. The customer was inconvenienced, and their expectations were perfection from their purchased product. It takes some strong inspiration to contend with that scenario day in and day out. Bill knows from where his inspiration comes.

An inspired individual must fully realize that some jobs of service are not sought out by *design,* but accepted by *default*. How many times have you ever heard of a child pulling on Mama's dress tail crying out,

"Mama! Mama! When I grow up, I wanna be a car salesman!"

"Mama! I can't wait 'til I grow up and wait tables at Cracker Barrel!" Now, for the readers that do not have the privilege to have a Cracker Barrel restaurant in your area, I am deeply saddened. I love a Cracker Barrel! I know of no other chain that has such consistency and continuity as Cracker Barrel.

Now, my being a resident of Tennessee, and worked in Lebanon, TN for a period, I have been privileged to enjoy the original Cracker Barrel store many times and honored to have known the founding owners. Of all the restaurants I've enjoyed, I have to say that Cracker Barrel has the friendliest servers of them all. They are not parrots spouting the common server phrases of most places. They don't ask what "we" are having today. They are real folks and, most often, very homey, down to earth, and friendly. Oh sure, anyone can have a bad day and be a little down, but by and large, the atmosphere is always upbeat and friendly. I love it!

Now, I must confess that I am extremely partial to servers as a whole, but I must say that our Cracker Barrel in Sevierville, TN is the best I have ever experienced and I am very protective of the servers there. They are the best! As I've mentioned before, our Smoky Mountains area is a grand tourist destination with millions of tourists visiting us each year. Those tourists come from all over the world to enjoy the beauty and wonder of these gorgeous Smoky Mountains and the family-friendly entertainment in our Sevierville-Pigeon Forge-Gatlinburg area.

It stands to reason that with so many different areas represented, there will be different expectations by the tourists. Our area servers have a daunting task. Servers catch a lot of flack when the eggs aren't cooked to the customer's expectation, or the grits (YES! We do eat grits in the South!) are a little runnier than you had hoped. There could be myriad of other minor problems that are not the server's fault.

117

The problems may have been the cook's miscue, or the input system failed. So, be kind to the server! They only take the order and deliver it. They cannot manage what they can't control. Don't shoot the messenger!

Now to the "after church" crowd on Sunday…. *Practice what you preach*! Your attitudes with these precious people are the worst of all! Every server with whom I have ever spoken tells the same story; they dread working the Sunday lunch crowd because church-goers are rude and contentious. Be *inspired* and display the Fruit Of The Spirit to your server. I can promise you that they did not come to work to be abused by the customers. Serving you is probably not their ideal lifelong goal. No one plans to be a server. There is a reason that they are there. Be *inspired*! Tip big!! Without them, it would be a buffet. And remember…

"Rudeness is a weak person's imitation of strength!"

I am reminded of this chorus which is a prayer that we all should pray:

"Make me a servant, humble and meek
Lord let me lift up those who are weak
And may the prayer of my heart always be
Make me a servant, Make me a servant today."
(Kelly Faye Willard – Maranatha Singers)

Servanthood: Making a loving choice for the betterment of another.

"For who is greater, the one who is at the table or the one who serves? Is it not the one who is at the table? But I am among you as one who serves."
(Luke 22:27)
118

MOTIVATION.... SERVITUDE

A certain degree of servitude exists in any employment relationship. There are responsibilities to the employer that exist simply because that is why one is hired to do a specific job that is an integral part of the corporate structure. We actively seek employment and should know what those responsibilities are. We should never confuse responsibility with servitude. Failing to meet our responsibilities as an employee is not an excuse to reason that we are under *servitude* and become hostile.

We are not forced to work for anyone. We *seek* employment. We are only forced to seek employment to satisfy the needs that we have to support our chosen lifestyle. We are not drafted by our employer. Too many people fault their employer for their poor performance. In that case, we put ourselves in a position of servitude by not being *inspired* to perform to the fullest as a result of our slothfulness or dissatisfaction. In other words, it all comes back to the choices that we have made.

Servitude is in direct contrast to *servanthood* in that servitude causes us to lose the loving choice to do something for the betterment of others. As an employed individual, it is imperative that we not confuse *responsibility* with *servitude*. Lack of responsibility (the sum total of our dismissive choices) will create an attitude exemplifying *motivation*. We are our own *motivator*; bad choices foster bad results. Can you really expect anything else?

It is very important to remember that within the employment arena we are expected to perform our duties to the fullest. If an individual is whining because the employer calls them out due to their lack of proper performance, it is the result of the choices that the employee has made which is the original *motivating circumstance*.

Don't feel as though you are a victim of being put under servitude if you haven't fulfilled your obligations. It might behoove you to decide to make proper choices concerning yourself which will break any bonds of personal bondage.

That being said, there are many other life circumstances that do foster a lifestyle of servitude that is not a matter of choice but circumstance: abusive parents, abusive spouses, abusive siblings, abusive religious practices, slave labor, bondage, victimization, and confinement.

Victims of these types of bondage suffer greatly; often in plain sight not showing signs of physical abuse but emotional and spiritual abuse showing no outward physical signs. Their countenance maybe downcast and show the body language of an oppressed individual. These individuals are being motivated by man and circumstance such that their spirit withdraws.

IF THIS IS YOU... PLEASE SEEK HELP! Talk to someone. It doesn't have to be a professional. Start with a trusted friend and pour out your heart to them and give that friend an opportunity to help you find your way back to a healthy lifestyle that will exhibit the Fruit Of The Spirit.

Don't be deceived by those that try to convince you that you are worthless. You were fearfully and wonderfully made, and God views you so precious to Him that he would sacrifice His Son for you. You needn't be in bondage to anyone or anything.

"It is for freedom that Christ has set us free. Stand firm, then, and do not let yourselves be burdened again by a yoke of slavery."
(Galatians 5:1)

Abundant Life or Abundant Strife

It is your choice....

It is Monday morning at the HotShot Motor Company, and it's time for that all-important, energy charged, Monday morning sales meeting and Mr. Ross, the dealer, is in fine form armed with a brand new incentive bonus plan for his sales staff. The faces of the staff reflect a common thought, "Here we go again. Oh, brother! Where is my coffee?"

"Good morning folks, I hope each of you had a great weekend and are rested and ready to hit the ground running today.

I am proud to announce a new incentive bonus plan for you that will give each of you the opportunity to make some extra money while garnering new clients that could be your customers as long as you are with us here at this dealership." (Humm? No hoorah intro? Gee, I wanted to shout "happy and healthy"….What's up with this?)

"I have realized that it is very important for every person here to have the opportunity to share in the bonuses and incentives that I design. This incentive is, of course, through a unified effort that doesn't create competition internally but creates a collective effort by each department to reach a designated goal. We must work together, not against each other. Every person should attain their proportionate share of the bonus amount based on their performance, coupled with their customer satisfaction reports. It is time we SERVE our customers and one another in this dealership family." (Oh my? Mr. Ross must be dying or something. Is he selling the dealership?)

"This dealership is made of many parts that, if finely tuned, can run as smooth as one of those new cars on the lot. But, just like that new car, every system is dependent on the other systems for it to operate smoothly and efficiently… and at full power." (Am I hearing him right?)

"Today will begin a new era here at the HotShot Motor Company with a re-branding of our name.

Today the sign will be changed to read the SURE SHOT MOTOR COMPANY reflecting the goal of providing our customers with absolute accuracy in every area of their purchase experience from front to back; incomparable service."

"Each month a percentage of the company gross profits will be shared with each employee based on their performance various areas. I will issue the ratios of performance and the respective reward system before day's end to each of you in the sales department and the other supportive departments as well. The success of this plan will be determined by a collective corporate endeavor to perform at an optimum pitch while serving our customers and our fellow employees before ourselves. (Oh my Lord, Mr. Ross has joined a cult!)

Now, this will not be like the Super Bowl; you will not get the ring just because you are on the team. Every incentive will be based on your personal performance and the synergistic excellence throughout the dealership.

Now, with that said, if you do not feel as though you can be an integral, operational part of this organization which strives for the common goal, I'd like to ask for a resignation letter by day's end. We will part as friends, but I desire to employ only those who are willing to be inspired, and not motivated, to perform with excellence here at SURE SHOT MOTOR COMPANY." (What in the world is he doing? He is going to lose some people that have been here for years. Maybe there are changes that have been needed for years, but why all of a sudden? What has come over him? It's that cult guru; I'll bet.)

"I have come to realize that for an entity to stand it must have a strong foundation and I am ready to ensure that we have the strongest foundation in the area. It begins with you... the sales staff. The entire dealership operates with the sale of a single car. If that experience is stellar for our customers, then the other departments will have to rise to the occasion as well. If the needs of our customer are met, then the dealership is and will be a continued success. No more treading water! We will have a destination." (Oh I bet we will have to wear uniforms!)

"Thank you for your attention, and I hope to see each of you here on the floor tomorrow where you will begin a new career of service to the community and one another. Thank you for your attention this morning."

As Mr. Ross begins to leave, he turns and says, "Brad…my office!"

After a brief stop by the accounting office, Mr. Ross enters his office and finds Brad waiting and thinking, "What have done now?"

"Brad, I've been thinking a lot about you lately…" (Oh no, here we go again!) "After our last discussion, I realized that my comments were falling off the table. I wanted to fire you up! However, it ended with you firing me up. You thanked me for a compliment that in no way meant to be a compliment, but a put-down. I said you were "TOO nice.""

I actually wanted to cause you to be more aggressive, but somehow you diffused my entire conversation when you said that you were "who you Mama raised you to be." I realized at that very moment that I was not who my Mama raised me to be, and it stung. It stung me hard.

Something (Spirit) came over me, and I realized that I had to change (conviction) the way I live and perceive life. I realized that your comments were the comments that every dealer could only dream to hear from their salespeople; steady performance, great customer service, and a willingness to be helpful to your fellow salespeople, in which you demonstrated with Rick's two deals last weekend."

"You have demonstrated exactly the spirit that I want to permeate this dealership. So, if you agree, I would like to promote you; not to the Sales Manager position, but I would like for you to become my General Manager of the entire dealership and lead this team to the Super Bowl. I want a sales floor full of people *just like you*. I want salespeople and customers that will last that have mutual respect and admiration for each other." I don't need a couple of racehorses. I need a team of evenly matched horses pulling in the same direction with the ability to go the distance. You, Brad, will hold the reins."

There you have it! Inspiration triumphs over Motivation! Mr. Ross was convicted to promote an atmosphere that would foster *inspiration* rather than *motivation*. Wow! What a positive change! Sure success is to follow by becoming servants to the community.

Whether it is a family, a corporate entity, a church, a ball team, a sewing circle, a Bible study group, or any collective scenario, if inspiration is flowing without the motivational distractions, great things can be accomplished.

But, where does it begin? It begins with you and the choices you make. Do you want *abundant life* or *abundant strife*?

Abundant life is the sum total of the inspired choices that you will make concerning every facet of your life. When you realize fully that dark and light cannot exist together, it becomes abundantly clear that to be inspired; one must operate in the Spirit for the Fruit Of The Spirit to operate. That fruit WILL NOT cohabitate with another spirit. It is impossible.

This begs the question once again, "What Spirit is living within you?" The answer to that question is paramount. If you are under the delusion that good works that are not initiated by the Holy Spirit will produce the Fruit Of The Spirit, you are woefully wrong. It will not happen... PERIOD.

The Holy Spirit cannot be imitated. The Holy Spirit will never sanction the fruit of the flesh. It is utterly impossible! The Fruit Of The Spirit and the fruit of the flesh cannot coexist. A choice is at hand

Abundant Life or Abundant Strife?

If you find that the Holy Spirit is not the spirit that lives within you, but you have realized that power of the Holy Spirit is your heart's desire to lead an inspired lifestyle, you will be glad to know that this gift is free of charge. However, for you to truly receive it, you must be *convicted by* the Holy Spirit, and not just *convinced* by this book or by any other means. You must seek His Spirit and the dynamics of *Inspiration* denouncing the world of M*otivation*.

It is impossible to manipulate God. It takes the surrender of your life to avail yourself of His power and enjoy a lifestyle of *Inspiration*.

So how do I receive this gift of the Holy Spirit? It is very simple. Just lose your life, as you know it, by accepting Jesus Christ as your personal Savior. You can't buy it or negotiate for it. Under the conviction of the Holy Spirit, losing your life to Christ opens the floodgates of heaven and the opportunity to have a personal relationship with the most powerful presence in the universe, our Heavenly Father, who through His Spirit, will guide and order your steps as you lead an inspired lifestyle.

That, my friend, is the gateway to *abundant life…* anything else will ensure a life of *abundant strife,* which is probably right where you are today. There will be no change. Don't expect it. Without the power and leading of the Holy Spirit to guide you, you are on your own. You are subject to the winds of every motivational tactic known to man.

As I mentioned at the beginning of this book, the primary purpose is to provide you with a Biblical method to "test the Spirit" of everything you think, say, or do, as well as being able to fend off the motivational tactics that are used against you by man and circumstance.

It is very important to realize that the Fruit Of The Spirit (Inspiration) produces a lifestyle that is without bondage...

"Against these things, there is no law." (Galatians 5:22)

But, the fruit of the flesh (Motivation) is finalized with the statement, "For those who live like this will not inherit the Kingdom of God" (Galatians 5:19)

Proof positive that one cannot expect to utilize *Inspiration* while living a lifestyle filled with *Motivation*.

Are you ready to begin an exciting lifestyle of Inspiration? If so...

"I urge you, brothers and sisters, in view of God's mercy, to offer your bodies as a living sacrifice, holy and pleasing to God—this is your true and proper worship.

Do not conform to the pattern of this world, but be transformed by the renewing of your mind. Then you will be able to test and approve what God's will is—his good, pleasing and perfect will."
(Romans 12:1)

The Bible tells me that if I love the Lord with all of my heart, He will give me the desires of my heart. My greatest desire is that you embrace a lifestyle of Inspiration as you conquer the forces of Motivation each day. *Abundant life or abundant strife*? It IS your choice. Choose wisely!

About The Author

Patrick Corn is a multi-faceted inspirational public speaker whose thirty years as a minister, corporate trainer, and concert level performer uniquely qualifies him to offer inspiring presentations for the church, corporate world, in sacred and secular convention venues.

His extensive radio broadcasts have been heard worldwide reaching millions with messages of insight, hope, and inspiration. His Smoky Mountain Cowboy Church broadcasts have been heard on both gospel and secular radio stations around the world.

Pat, a native of Hendersonville, NC, has also enjoyed a robust career in the music industry as a concert level performer, vocalist, composer, and arranger. Educated at North Texas State University, where he majored in Jazz arranging and composition, he relocated to the Nashville area in 1975 where he served the music industry extensively and entered his ministry efforts in 1981. 1994 brought a stirring to return to the mountains. He and his beautiful wife Monica, and two daughters Ashley and Amber moved to the Great Smoky Mountains to essentially retire from the music industry. His family lives in Sevierville, TN where his ministry continues along with other business pursuits.

Dr. Corn is a co-founder of "Life-Support"... a Solution Focused Life Coaching-Counseling-Consulting practice for developing personal growth and life goal attainment for personal and corporate clients.

He proudly partners with daughter Ashley Bergman who is a marriage and family therapist and adjunct professor at a local university. Their practice serves both personal clientele and business clientele in the local East Tennessee area as well as online.

His live presentations are available for churches, corporate training, and conventions of all types, seeking to inspire the attendees to develop a proactive lifestyle through a life of inspiration.

Please visit
www.patcornministries.com
and
www.life-support.life

for more information concerning his live presentations, workshops, and ministry opportunities for you personally, your church, or your business.

Always timely with one goal...
to "Light Him Up!"

Presentations
For Churches, Conferences, and Corporate Workshops.

"Inspiration vs Motivation."
This presentation illuminates the contrast between inspiration and motivation. It provides an opportunity for the listener to gain control of the choices that they make in their personal life and professional life creating a pro-active lifestyle which fosters greater productivity. This presentation has been deemed as "life-changing."

"Whom The Father Seeks"
Developing a daily lifestyle of true worship and how to become the individual that the Father is seeking.

This dynamic presentation is perfect for adults and teens. WTFS will teach, with pinpoint accuracy, how to become a worshiper who worships "in Spirit and in truth." This is the kind of worshiper that the Father is seeking. Become a "True Worshiper."

"One Guy- One Guitar-One God"
Discovering the Object of true worship.

This presentation will direct your attention to the true Object of personal and corporate worship with a very simple process. It is suitable for any age group and will bring Romans 12:1 to a stark reality. This presentation is a suitable for a congregational service or as a workshop for the music ministry of the church as a preparatory function.

"Headlock"
Tearing down the strongholds of life.

This presentation is suitable for all age groups at church or school conferences. This presentation addresses the strongholds that young and old suffer in their personal lives. It presents a proven method to break the headlock that life, as they perceive it, has on them. He presentation illuminates what is normal, and what is abnormal, in a Christ-center lifestyle while dealing with the pressures that the world imposes.

This presentation has a very desirable aspect in that it can be planned to afford the attendees a personal, one-on-one session to discuss the strongholds in their lives. The sole purpose is to break the strongholds that they are experiencing and allow them to experience freedom from the bondage that has put a chokehold on their life.

Special guests are often utilized when this program is offered as a two or three-day workshop and clinic.

Other presentations are available that will be very productive for your personal and business growth. Please contact Dr. Corn through the websites provided below. Your request will be addressed quickly and personally.

www.patcornministries.com

www.life-support.life

97449190R00086

Made in the USA
Columbia, SC
14 June 2018